PEOPLE SKILLS
FOR ANALYTICAL
THINKERS

Boost Your Communication and
Advance Your Career - and Life

GILBERT EIJKELENBOOM

Praise for
People Skills for Analytical Thinkers

★ ★ ★ ★ ★

"For the engineer, scientist, or technology professional seeking to communicate better in the business world, this is the book you've been craving your entire career!"

— **Douglas Laney**, *Innovation Fellow, West Monroe, and best-selling author of "Infonomics"*

★ ★ ★ ★ ★

"As a cognitive observer of others and an analytical thinker, I was always puzzled that there must be some sort of underlying neural mechanism that leads us to speak or act the way we do in response to various situations. Gilbert has solved that puzzle for me in this wonderful book."

— **Kirk Borne**, *Data Scientist. Astrophysicist. Global Speaker. Top Influencer.*

★ ★ ★ ★ ★

"A timely exploration into the connection between logical thinking and emotional intelligence, and the value of developing and enriching soft skills for the analytical thinker. Data and analytics professionals will benefit from the research-intensive insights into this frequently overlooked, yet increasingly relevant, vehicle for driving productivity, transformation, and interpersonal fulfillment."

— **Ronald van Loon**, *CEO, Principal Analyst at Intelligent World, Global Top 10 AI, Big Data & Analytics influencer*

★ ★ ★ ★ ★

"Gilbert's book is the rare piece that translates the idea of 'soft skills' in a tangible, practical and actionable way. Practitioners, leaders, and those interested in bring themselves to their work will find immense value in this book!"

— **Eric Weber**, *Head of Experimentation, Yelp*

★ ★ ★ ★ ★

"*People Skills for Analytical Thinkers* is much needed resource for the analytics professional wanting to create more impact in their work. Often relegated as warm and fuzzy, Gilbert has done a masterful job at highlighting the importance of 'soft skills' that often get overlooked in data and analytics. If you want to position yourself for success and add one more tool in your toolbox this year, work on your ability to communicate and influence. Gilbert shines a light where this might be for you."

— **Gregory Nelson**, *AVP Analytics, Intermountain Healthcare, Author of: The Analytics Lifecycle Toolkit"*

★ ★ ★ ★ ★

"As I was reading *People Skills for Analytical Thinkers* I found myself nodding and smiling at passages on nearly every page. I was painfully shy when I was in high school, but made the decision that I was going to change my approach to social interactions and how I put myself out in the world. Gilbert's book is a great roadmap for those who are comfortable relating to data, math and algorithms, but want to be more at ease in their social interactions. I enjoyed the book and I can see how it can make a significant difference for many of our analytically oriented colleagues. I recommend it highly."

— **John K. Thompson**, *Global Head, Advanced Analytics & Artificial Intelligence, CSL Behring*

★ ★ ★ ★ ★

"I highly recommend this book, especially for Data Science professionals. To drive true innovation and impact, in this Age of Artificial Intelligence, it is critical to get both things right: algorithms and implementation. For the latter, the ideas and the recipes Gilbert has provided in this book are invaluable."

— **Priyo Chatterjee**, *Founder and Principal, AiLytica, Author of "Analytics in the Age of Artificial Intelligence" (forthcoming)*

★ ★ ★ ★ ★

"Today's digital leaders must master the left brain and right brain aspects of leadership. Gilbert's book guides left brain dominant individuals into a mastery of their right brain skills in order to become a more well-rounded leader. This book is a must read for analytics thinkers seeking to progress in their career"

— **R "Ray' Wang**, *Best-selling Author and CEO of Constellation Research, Inc.*

People Skills for Analytical Thinkers

by Gilbert Eijkelenboom

Published by MindSpeaking

www.MindSpeaking.com

© 2020 Gilbert Eijkelenboom

TABLE OF CONTENTS

FOREWORD

For analytical thinkers, the future has never been brighter. Minds like yours are the driving force of the fourth industrial revolution. While technology and data are driving this revolution, these skills alone will not be enough to help us seize the opportunity this transformation presents. In an age of AI and automation, there is one skill that will continue to grow in importance: people skills.

With attention spans continuing to get shorter, being able to concisely deliver your message and influence people is of upmost importance. I make this statement with great confidence, having spent the majority of my career building out numerous greenfield analytics teams. I have experienced what does and does not work in terms of communicating clearly to influence and drive change.

People skills are an essential component of the formula for professional success. The fact that you are reading this book signifies that you also embrace this idea. Adopting and practicing the concepts and strategies presented here is one of the best investments you can make in yourself.

Soon after meeting Gilbert for the first time, I realized that he had an exceptional portfolio of real-world experience and expertise on this topic. In this book, he translates his vast experience and proficiency into a playbook that people can use to develop their communication and people skills in a logical and pragmatic manner.

As an analytical thinker, you may enjoy challenging other people's perspectives with your analytical insights. In the same way, Gilbert challenges you to think about the way you communicate. From understanding your internal algorithms to how you can influence other people, he outlines a transformational path that will drive your personal and professional growth. The end goal of this book is to give you the tools and frameworks to be clearly heard, effectively communicate your message with confidence, and influence people.

Analytical thinkers with people skills are a powerful force. They are an extraordinarily scarce, valuable, and impactful resource for organizations. They have the ability to drive real change. Additionally, they can do almost anything they wish in their careers because these skills are so versatile. This book represents your movement toward this future.

I passionately believe that the abilities discussed in this book are game-changers. I support the work that Gilbert is doing and believe that you will find this book an immensely valuable resource that you will come back to time and time again. I also encourage you to check out Gilbert's training program for data professionals. His soft skills workshops serve as an extension of the foundational ideas discussed in this book.

To properly set expectations, learning these people skills is not an easy endeavor. However, nothing worthwhile comes easy. Lucky for you, you have this amazing resource to help you improve these skills quickly and reliably.

People skills not only help you to improve your performance at work — they are also life skills that will help you become a better person. Embrace the process and watch your growth take off. The future you will thank you.

Jason Krantz

CEO Strategy Titan

INTRODUCTION

I've just lost $45,000 playing online poker. Ouch. All of that money wasted in one night. I imagine the trip around the world I could have taken instead. From the Carnival in Rio de Janeiro to skydiving in Sydney. From tuna sashimi in Tokyo to hiking in the Himalayas. Everything flushed down the drain. I feel frustrated. Angry with the cards. Disappointed with myself.

I'm still clicking my mouse, but my mind has long since switched off. Slowly, the sun rises and peeks through the blinds of my student flat. I'm exhausted. The only thing that keeps me awake is my unwillingness to accept my record loss.

That was September 2, 2009. For 2 years, I played online poker at a professional level. I loved it. I still see myself sitting behind my 30-inch monitor, smiling. In online poker, I could optimize every decision based on statistics. When I clicked on a player's icon, a window with 120 different numbers appeared, which helped me understand how the other person plays.

Poker is a game of analysis and math. That's why I was good at it. The thing is, real life is more than analysis. Human interaction is different from math. You cannot optimize social situations by taking the derivative. On the contrary, the more I analyzed, the more I screwed up. "Does this person like me?" "What should I say next?" "Is this good, smart, funny enough?" I was always overthinking. Also, I was shy, and that led to awkward situations.

I will never forget one day in my first year of university. We were sitting in a small group to agree on the next steps for our project. Like always, I had been mostly silent. Then suddenly, a girl in the group asked, "Gilbert, do you agree?" Before I could open my mouth, another guy said, "He doesn't have an opinion anyway." The guy smiled at me. I just looked at him, not knowing what to say. There were no statistics above his head that told me how to respond. The only response I could come up with was a poker face. I didn't show anything on the outside. But on the inside, it felt like the guy had twisted a knife in my heart.

While the group conversation proceeded, I zoomed out. I looked at my watch, counting down the minutes of the meeting while I thought, "This is not how I want to live..." Something had to change, but I had no idea where to start.

Challenges of Analytical Thinkers

Back then, I didn't realize it, but now I know I wasn't the only one struggling. Many people overthink things in social situations. In the years before writing this book, I got so passionate about the challenges of these analytical thinkers that I wanted to know everything about them. That's why I interviewed:

- **118** analytical thinkers
- **45** people in business roles who work with analytical thinkers
- **3** psychologists

I define "analytical thinkers" as individuals who state that at least 10 out of the following 20 words describe their character. How many do you recognize in yourself?

Analytical	Rational
Cautious	Reflective
Deliberate	Scientific
Discreet	Serious
Exact	Statistical
Introverted	Systematic
Logical	Technical
Intellectual	Thinker
Mathematical	Thorough
Methodical	Process-oriented

From the interviews I held, I discovered that many analytical thinkers struggle with the same challenges. Most of these challenges relate to soft skills: people's ability to communicate with each other and work well together.[1] In the current era of technology, your analytical skills are incredibly valuable. But you may have found that it's challenging to communicate with people who don't have the same level of analytical skills. And that's where soft skills come in handy. But are there other reasons why soft skills are important in your career? Let's ask Deloitte, McKinsey, and the academic world.

Why should you care about soft skills?

Research by Deloitte (2019) shows that the jobs in highest demand today and those with the highest acceleration in salaries are so-called "hybrid jobs".[2] Hybrid jobs bring together technical skills with soft skills, such as communication and collaboration.

The 2018 LinkedIn Workplace Learning Report presented similar findings: training for soft skills is the number one priority. The report highlights communication (#2) and collaboration (#3) among the most important soft skills to learn.[3]

McKinsey observed this trend as well. According to a paper from McKinsey Global Institute (2018) on automation and the future of the workforce, demand for social and emotional skills will increase by 24% by 2030, compared to 2016. The paper stated, "The demand for soft skills is beginning to surge."[4]

Katy Börner, a distinguished professor of engineering and information science, drew a parallel conclusion. From the academic research that Börner led and published in 2018, they found that "in an increasingly data-driven economy, the demand for 'soft' social skills, like teamwork and communication, increase with greater demand for 'hard' technical skills and tools."[5]

If you aren't yet motivated to develop your soft skills, I'll give you three more reasons why it's a good idea to start today:

1) Soft skills are relevant in every job that requires collaboration with others.

2) Technology is continually changing. Some of the programming languages that were in high demand in the past are about to go extinct. In contrast, soft skills will always stay relevant.

3) Soft skills help you in all areas in your life, whether it's to make new friends, improve your dating life, or deepen the relationships with your family.

Have you ever been rejected for a job, passed over for promotion, or seen as "too serious" by the people around you? In that case, more advanced soft skills would have made your world look different.

In this book, I use the term "people skills" because it's clear that these skills are all about people. Namely, the ability to communicate and collaborate with other people and the ability to influence them. Your people skills might be well-developed. Or perhaps you're at the start of your journey. In either case, I have been in your shoes.

My transformation

While I was playing poker, I thought I faced many tough decisions. Should I make a small bet and hope the other guy won't call my bluff? Or should I shove all my poker chips to the middle, risking the equivalent of a four-week holiday?

Tough choices. But in the third year of my studies, I had a decision of a different order in front of me. Three friends — fellow poker players — decided to move to Malta for a year. They asked me if I wanted to move in with them. A beautiful apartment near the beach, in a country free of poker taxes. How tempting.

Should I bet on poker? Or go all-in on another direction in my life?

After a lot of thinking — because, yes, that's who I am — I decided not to go to Malta. Instead, I quit poker completely. Looking back, I'm happy I did. It turned out to be the start of a transformation. I decided I wanted to get better at interacting with people and started experimenting.

Instead of raising a bet on the poker table, I raised my voice in social situations. Instead of covering my cards, I strived to be more open. Instead of hiding my emotions behind a poker face, I tried to express them.

Along my journey, I have read over sixty books on human behavior. The books were helpful, but they never taught me how the lessons applied to analytical thinkers. That's why I started trying out new things. It was hard. I failed miserably. Many times. But step by step, I got a little better at interacting with others. And, importantly, I discovered a systematic approach to improve my people skills as an analytical thinker. A way to benefit from my logical mind, instead of having it block my potential to connect with others.

I can still feel the pain when I think about the remark that the guy in my university group made. But fortunately, everything has changed. When I see a room full of new people, I can enter with a smile, instead of having my legs shake from anxiety. Now, after my transformation, colleagues see my interpersonal skills as my biggest strength. Nowadays, I get up much, much happier than I did before I started working on my people skills.

Anyway, it's not about me. It's about *you.*

I'm only telling you my story to demonstrate that you can do the same. As I have experienced these challenges firsthand, I know how hard human interactions can be as an analytical thinker. That's why I would love to help you advance your people skills.

How this book will help you

When you work on your people skills, you will develop the desirable profile that researchers from McKinsey and others are talking about. As a result, your next promotion and salary increase will soon knock on your door. While no one hates a pay raise, I would say that the personal gains are more important. People skills help you gain confidence and create smooth social interactions. Imagine meeting a group of people you don't know. Often, this means a lot of forced small talk. However, people skills allow you to steer a dull dialogue into an interesting conversation.

The tools in this book will help you grow your emotional intelligence, which is a crucial skill in building fulfilling relationships with colleagues, friends, and family. Through the exercises, you will also increase your influence, have people listen to your ideas, and get more freedom to work on the projects you enjoy the most. Lastly, perhaps surprisingly, you will see that emotional intelligence is an amazing cure against indecisiveness.

Understanding human behavior is not easy. But it gets unnecessarily complex when someone explains psychology in terms that don't fit your way of thinking. That's why this book is not packed with fluffy descriptions about human relationships. Instead, this book takes an analytical approach to your own and other people's behavior. While you can pick your friends, you cannot choose your colleagues. And that leads to challenging situations. That's why this book pays most attention to social interactions at work. Nevertheless, improving your people skills in a work setting has tremendous benefits in your personal life too.

I will guide you through a new framework with 26 principles for improving your people skills as an analytical person, using a combination of academic research, exercises, and real-life office stories. I have put my heart into this book and will share painful mistakes that I have made. Every now and then, you will see the page bleed. This is the book I wish I could have read when I started my career.

This book consists of four parts:

Part 1 – BE SELF-AWARE:

- Understanding your own behavioral patterns, making interactions with others easier, more productive, and more fun
- Understanding and expressing your emotions and learning how that increases your influence

Part 2 – OPTIMIZE:

- Reprogramming your mind and getting results that make you proud
- Expressing clear boundaries and saying no while taking other people's feelings into account

Part 3 – INTERACT:

- Boosting your people skills by increasing your empathy and social confidence
- Improving your communication and collaboration with colleagues; yes, even with your emotionally explosive coworkers
- Learning how to deal with small-talk conversations you don't enjoy

Part 4 – INFLUENCE:

- Steering people's behavior while you improve relationships
- Developing your negotiation skills and getting the freedom to work on projects you enjoy the most
- Having others take your ideas seriously and seeing the impact of your work in the end result
- Becoming a master persuader by avoiding the single mistake that almost everyone makes

PART 1

BE SELF-AWARE: UNDERSTAND YOUR OWN ALGORITHMS

INTRODUCTION

Every day, there are thousands of situations in which you make a decision:

- Why did you decide to buy that piece of chocolate at 3:00 p.m.?
- What made you go to the gym yesterday?
- How did you respond this morning when that man cut the line at the coffee shop?

Some decisions relate directly to your work:

- Why did you not speak up when you had that new idea?
- What made you offer your help to that colleague?
- How did you respond when your colleague got that promotion instead of you?

All the decisions you've made in the past determine where you are in your life right now. For big decisions, such as what to study, where to work, and where to live, it's obvious that they have a big impact on your life. In contrast, the decisions in the previous bullet points may seem insignificant. However, as we will see, these smaller choices can have a big impact on your life too.

Despite this impact, much of our daily behavior is based on unconscious decisions. On the one hand, this is good, because it would be exhausting to think extensively about every minor choice. On the other hand, there is a big disadvantage, because a lack of awareness may lead to undesirable results. This first part of the book focuses on increasing your self-awareness.

CHAPTER 1:
YOUR BRAIN AS A SET OF ALGORITHMS

Imagine you're driving a car at a high speed while you approach a red traffic light. When do you push the brake? This primary question has many secondary questions underneath that determine the answer.

- What is your speed?

- How far away are the cars in front of you?

- What is the chance that the traffic light will turn green before you get there?

- If you brake too early, is there a chance you will miss the green light and be late for your appointment?

- If you brake too late, is there enough space between the car in front of you to avoid a crash?

- What is the preference of your child in the back, who has car sickness?

- How will people in cars behind you respond if you brake at the last second?

- What kind of driver do you want to be?

You process many of these questions unconsciously. How does that work? You aren't aware of it, but in each situation, you take in many variables. These variables are the input for your decision. This input is then processed by your brain, which determines what the response should be. The response is the output: your behavior in that situation.

You can see your brain as a set of algorithms. Every situation we are in has many different variables. These form the input of our algorithms. This input is processed by the algorithm that is appropriate to the situation. Then, that algorithm produces an output: our behavior.

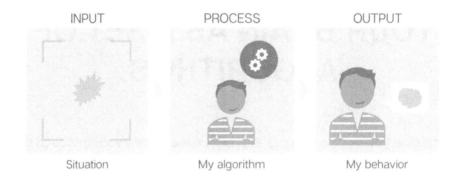

INPUT	PROCESS	OUTPUT
Situation	My algorithm	My behavior

Principle #1:

You can see your brain as a set of algorithms. All situational variables are taken as input and processed into an output. In other words, our algorithms analyze a situation and tell us what to do.

Each part of this book zooms in on one element of this illustration. Part 1 starts right at the center — I will explain how you can become more aware of your own algorithms.

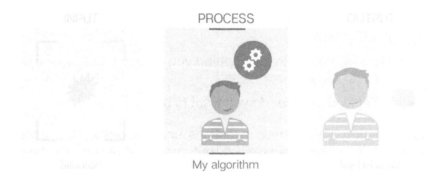

PROCESS

My algorithm

The situation in the car example has many factual variables (speed, distance to next car, duration of green light). Therefore, your optimal response can mostly be calculated. However, there are a few emotional variables as well (child with car sickness, impact on people in other cars).

Situations in your personal and professional life are full of emotional variables that don't have a binary answer. It's difficult to understand how these variables are processed. Give me a scientific situation and I will apply physics and math, then I will give you the answer. Add people with emotions and it gets tricky. Do you recognize this? The more people are involved, the more the complex decision-making becomes, because emotional variables are mostly unknown and difficult to model quantitatively. Moreover, everyone processes these variables in a different way through their personal algorithms.

Your algorithms help you make quick decisions in daily life. However, when you aren't aware of how both factual and emotional variables are processed, many of your decisions aren't optimal. For example, I find it difficult to say no to people. At times, my algorithms suggest helping someone else, even when I don't want to. If I blindly follow my algorithms, my own work or personal life suffers.

When you are unaware of your own algorithms, they may produce an output that doesn't make you perform well at work, or simply doesn't make you happy. Fortunately, there is a clear solution: emotional intelligence.

CHAPTER 2: EMOTIONAL INTELLIGENCE

As I mentioned in the last chapter, you can see your brain as a group of algorithms. Your algorithms help you process situations, and based on that, you decide how you will behave. This decision-making process doesn't only look at facts and figures. Emotions are also an important part of the equation.

The brain has two systems to process situations into behavior:

1) Limbic system — the emotional brain

2) Neocortex — the rational brain

Together, they are the driving force behind your algorithms. Daniel Kahneman, who won the Nobel Prize in Economics in 2001, calls them "system 1" and "system 2".[6] Nothing but respect for his work in behavioral economics, but could he not have come up with more memorable names? Well, maybe Kahneman thought it wouldn't get any better than the analogy that Jonathan Haidt came up with. This social psychologist saw the two systems as an elephant and a rider. The elephant is emotional, irrational, and impulsive. On the other side, the rider is analytical, rational, and controlled. The rider objectively knows the best way to go, but the elephant is 70 times heavier. The rider can gently steer and pull the elephant in a direction (rational brain), but the elephant goes where they want to go (emotional brain).[7]

The classic (and false) assumption is this: disregard feelings; only focus on facts.[8] That is exactly how I thought six years ago. However, if you eliminate emotions, you ignore the beast that has all the power.

Have you ever:

1) Said to yourself that you would work out more often, only to find your butt on the couch watching TV?

2) Decided to address a colleague who disturbs you with his loud phone call, then stayed silent at your desk?

3) Decided to ask your boss for a raise, but let months pass by without any action?

These are all examples of your emotional elephant at work. There is one major reason why we are often not aware that our emotional elephant has a lot of influence. In these cases, your rational rider knows what is best for you, but your emotional elephant enjoys instant gratification and pushes for the easy path. The rider cannot tame the elephant, but finds it difficult to admit that they are not in control. That's why your rider will try to find a logical justification:

1) "Skipping the gym once doesn't hurt."

2) "He's probably almost done calling. It's not that loud anyways."

3) "After summer is probably a better time to ask for a raise. And compared to my friends' salaries, my salary isn't that bad."

You become powerful when you can tap into both your rational brain and your emotional brain. The rider and the elephant need to work in harmony. And that's where emotional intelligence comes into play.

According to Daniel Goleman, an internationally known psychologist, the definition of emotional intelligence is, "The ability to recognize, understand and manage our own emotions; and to recognize, understand and influence the emotions of others."[9]

Whether you like it or not, emotions will influence how you make decisions. Next to factual variables, emotional variables are always part of your algorithms. Remember how strong your emotional elephant is — this massive animal heavily impacts your decisions. Therefore, the better you understand what makes your emotions go up and down, the better you understand your algorithms. And the better you understand your algorithms, the easier the interactions with other people become. Embrace emotions and use them to your advantage.

Emotions are crucial in your life, even if you still think that feelings don't play a role in your decision-making. Why? Because you interact with people every day. And most of those people have an enormous elephant, much bigger than its rider. You can try to convince someone with the best and most logical argument you can think of. However, if you don't listen to the other person's emotional brain, you will have a hard time changing their mind. In his 1996 book, Goleman shows that neglecting emotions in the workplace harms your effectiveness.

Antonio Damasio, a neuroscientist, also found out about the importance of emotions. One of his patients, Elliott, had suffered damage to the frontal lobes of his brain due to a tumor. Elliott had a prosperous life. He was an intelligent and diplomatic man — a role model to his colleagues. After the surgery, however, Elliott began to have trouble managing his day. Whenever he tried to accomplish something, he would lose focus. He spent hours deciding where to have lunch, and still could not choose. Then Elliott lost his job and wasted his life savings on foolish investments. He divorced his wife, married a woman his family disapproved of, and quickly divorced again. In short, he was incapable of making sensible choices.

To find out what happened, Damasio did a series of tests. The results showed that Elliott had a superior IQ, an excellent memory for numbers, and did well making estimates based upon incomplete information. However, Damasio noticed something: Elliott never showed any emotions.

In another test, Damasio showed Elliott lots of traumatic images, like pictures of burning buildings and gruesome accidents. After the test, Elliot told Damasio that those images used to give him strong emotions, but now he didn't feel anything. A series of further tests showed that Elliott could perfectly line up all pros and cons of a complex decision. What Elliott could not do was actually make the choice. Other research subjects of Damasio, who also lost emotional functions through brain surgery, demonstrated the same inability to make decisions.[10]

Dr. Travis Bradberry, author of *Emotional Intelligence 2.0*, echoes the findings of Damasio with a thought-provoking quote, "The most logical decision-making pays attention to emotions."[11]

When I started my career as a consultant at Cognizant, I saw myself as a rational person. I proudly told others that I preferred to make decisions based on numbers and rational analysis. I said, "Emotions stir up the mathematical equation; feelings should be avoided to come to the best possible conclusion." Fast-forward to today and I am still an advocate of rational decision-making in many situations. However, now I understand that, sometimes, emotions can be valuable pieces of data. Life is complex, and we never have a complete set of information. Analysis seldom gives us clear-cut decisions. In most situations, the best that logic can do is present us with several possible options. Emotions can help us recognize our inner desires and make a good choice.

Then, how can you understand something so elusive like your emotions? By developing a good connection with your emotional elephant. Even though your emotional elephant is impulsive, every now and then, it demonstrates a strong intuition in the right way to go. By contrast, the rational rider only has a map that shows facts about the different paths. Your goal is not to tame the elephant. Instead, your goal is to become friends. That doesn't mean, however, that you should *always* follow the advice of your new companion.

Imagine you're at work and your manager asks your team who wants to volunteer to give a presentation next week. You are interested in the topic, but you feel some tension in your stomach. What does that mean?

1) Is your emotional elephant pushing for shortcuts, giving irrelevant reasons?

   For example, "Do not do the presentation. You may be excited for this opportunity, but this is going to be way too scary."

Or,

2) Is your emotional elephant telling you something valuable?

   For example, "You have a lot on your plate already. And your other projects mean much more to you."

In the first case, you may decide to push through the fear and volunteer for the presentation. In the second case, you could decide to pass up the opportunity to ensure that you focus on what is most important to you. This is how your emotional elephant and rational rider form a partnership: they both play a role in your decision-making. As a result, you develop powerful algorithms that take both sides into account: both facts and emotions.

Emotions do matter. Emotions can be useful. However, that doesn't mean you should always blindly follow them. Increasing your emotional intelligence helps you understand when it's a good idea to listen.

Principle #2:

Even as a rational person, your emotions are crucial for the decisions you make in your life. Learn how to recognize your own and other people's emotions and use them to your advantage.

CHAPTER 3:
HOW ALGORITHMS
ARE FORMED

At times, emotions can help us make better decisions. While you can benefit from your emotional brain today, its role was even more important thousands of years ago. Back then, the emotional brain was crucial for survival. Why? Responses from the emotional brain are milliseconds faster than responses from the rational brain. As cavemen, it wasn't useful to overanalyze when you faced a saber-tooth tiger. An instant emotional reaction to trigger a Usain Bolt sprint was a more optimal response.

As caveman, we faced more dangers: abandonment from the group had serious consequences. If you weren't liked by your social group, you were kicked out of the tribe. That meant no food and no shelter. Rejection by the group wasn't just painful like today. Rejection was deadly. Still, today, people have a strong need to belong and even stronger aversion to be rejected.[12] Even though tribe hierarchy isn't that important anymore, we're still sensitive to getting along well with others. Thanks to millions of years of evolution, we have developed a strong fear of social rejection. That's why we get irrationally nervous for a presentation, thinking "What if the group doesn't like it?"

Principle #3:

Thanks to evolution, our brain is wired to look out for rejection. As a result, we are irrationally sensitive in our need to belong to others.

Unfortunately, because our brain is hardwired by evolution, our outdated fears still have a negative effect on our job performance today. The question is how you deal with it. Do you let your outdated fears rule your life? Or do you realize that we're not cavemen anymore and start to optimize your algorithms today?

Evolution has a large impact on our decisions today. Keeping this knowledge in the back of our mind, how are our algorithms formed throughout our life?

Many of our algorithms have been created during childhood. As a child, we are full of curiosity and enjoy exploring the world. We are wired to try out everything in our environment, because that's how we learn about the world. The repeated experiences are the basis for behavioral patterns. We internalize these patterns and use them as a template for similar situations in the future: an algorithm is formed!

John Bowlby, a famous psychologist, calls this template for the social world an "internal working model."[13] You can see this internal working model as an algorithm that tells us what to do in different situations.

To make this more concrete, let me give you a few childhood examples.

EXAMPLE 1: hug

I start crying. My mother comes and hugs me. I like it.

As a baby, I see the following if/then statement:

If I want a hug from my mom, then I will cry.

* BLEEP — algorithm formed *

The algorithm looks like:

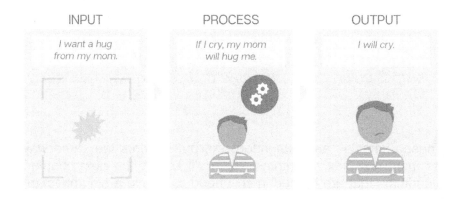

EXAMPLE 2: oven

The oven is turned on. I touch the oven. It hurts. I don't like it.

As a kid, I see the following if/then statement:

If the oven is turned on, then I won't touch it.

* BLEEP — algorithm formed *

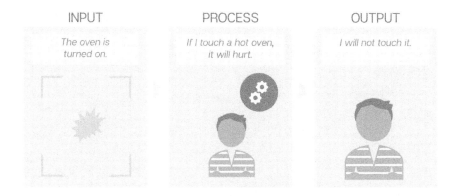

Our algorithms are formed through positive and negative reinforcement. After we choose our behavior, we are rewarded (hug) or punished (burn). In some situations, we internalize an algorithm after seeing it play out once. In other cases, we only adopt the optimal behavior after burning our fingers 10 times — literally or figuratively.

Principle #4:

Algorithms are formed through our experiences in the world. We embed a belief about the optimal output given different types of input. In other words, we learn how we should behave in different types of situations.

These examples are straightforward, but it works the same way for more complex algorithms. As you'll see in the next chapter, algorithms that are formed in childhood can have a big impact on your professional life.

CHAPTER 4:
HARMFUL ALGORITHMS

Parents in Conflict

By not touching the oven, you avoid pain. Useful pattern to learn, right? Absolutely. However, that doesn't mean all algorithms you form in your childhood bring you desirable results.

Let me give you a personal example from 1998. I was sitting on the sofa watching TV and my well-organized dad entered the room. He liked an orderly space. My dad saw a pile of papers on the living room table, which my mom left there a few minutes earlier. He raised his voice, "Why can you not ever keep your stuff tidy? You don't have any system for organizing your life."

My messy and creative mom replied, "I put these things here five minutes ago. Why can you not say anything positive?"

The next thing I saw was my parents sitting far away from each other with angry faces. To the nine-year-old me, they seemed not to like each other. What made it more complicated is that my parents enjoyed having heated political debates. As a young child, I didn't recognize the difference between a debate and a fight. What I did recognize was the result: angry faces and disconnection. Therefore, in my young mind, even healthy disagreements led to people not liking each other.

After being the observer of these disagreements many times, I internalized the following belief:

If I openly disagree with someone, **then** the other person will be angry with me, and they won't like me.

I didn't want the other person to be angry. And I did want others to like me.

That's why I created the following algorithm for myself:

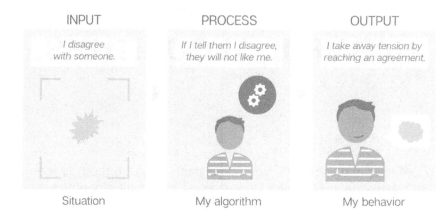

INPUT	PROCESS	OUTPUT
I disagree with someone.	If I tell them I disagree, they will not like me.	I take away tension by reaching an agreement.
Situation	My algorithm	My behavior

I learned how to deal with situations of tension: steer away from them, even if it means withholding thoughts and compromising on my standpoint. My emotional elephant chooses the easy path: avoiding a confrontation.

As a result of the algorithm I formed, I've made many suboptimal choices in my professional and personal life:

1) I've said "I agree," when I didn't support a decision.

2) I've said "It's fine to go with your idea" when deep inside, I wasn't fine.

3) I've told myself "It's not that bad" when someone crossed my boundaries.

This gave me the short-term results I was looking for: a happy face and a feeling of connection. However, in the long term, this created a few problems:

1) I was less motivated to work when I didn't agree with the vision of the project.

2) I had good ideas, but because I didn't have the courage to speak up, people didn't know about them.

3) I was angry at the other person for crossing my boundaries, while I was mad at myself for not expressing boundaries. This resentment made me unhappy.

Saying no

Since I thought that tension in social situations would always lead to angry people and disconnection, I also found it difficult to say no. I felt that I had to avoid saying no to stay away from tension.

INPUT	PROCESS	OUTPUT
Someone asks me for help.	*If I say no, the other person will not like me.*	*I will avoid saying no.*

Again, I've made many suboptimal choices in my professional and personal life:

1) I've said yes when I didn't have enough time.

2) I've said yes when I was too tired.

3) I've said "maybe later" when I really meant no.

Again, I got great short-term results: happy faces and a feeling of connection. But the long-term results were less joyful:

1) I came in late to appointments because I was finishing a request for someone else.

2) I felt angry with other people because they made an "unreasonable" request. However, the only person I was actually angry with was myself — for saying yes.

3) People found it hard to understand what I really meant. I wasn't clear.

Paradoxically, by saying yes, I got the results I was most afraid of: an angry face and a feeling of disconnection.

Now I understand better how my algorithm works and how I can choose a different behavior. I have experienced that saying no can build relationships rather than tear them apart. And, hey, my parents are still happily together — so this shows that a strong disagreement doesn't need to lead to disconnection.

Changing algorithms that you formed in your childhood isn't easy, but the rewards are tremendous. We'll look at how you can change your own algorithms in Part 2: Optimize.

These algorithms, which I built in my childhood, still impacted my life many years later. I'm not the only one. Everyone — yes, everyone — builds algorithms in their childhood.

Maybe you could see yourself in some of the examples I presented earlier. Or maybe you were thinking about other examples: algorithms that *you* formed in your childhood. That's exactly what we're going to explore next. While reading the following two examples, I would like you to think "How does this remind me of a situation in my own childhood?"

Tony's train track

Tony is seven years old and is playing with his electrical train. He builds a new train track so he can pick up people in the village and bring them to their work. Tony wonders if he can carry out the same in the real world. He feels smart, because in this way, people don't need to take the car anymore. Less cars on the highway — no more traffic jams. Proudly, he runs to his dad and says, "Daddy, I have a great idea!"

His dad, reading the newspaper, briefly looks up, annoyed that his son is interrupting his Sunday readings. Tony is confused but still shows his dad the train track, telling him about his idea.

The dad says to Tony, "You aren't solving the world here, smart-ass. That already exists. Also, nobody likes sitting in a crowded train." After making this remark, he goes back to reading the newspaper.

Tony feels disappointed. When this situation is repeated over time, Tony creates the following belief:

If I express my idea, **then** people will think I'm annoying and won't like me.

To prevent this painful experience from happening again in the future (because remember, we want to be liked and belong to our tribe), he forms the following algorithm:

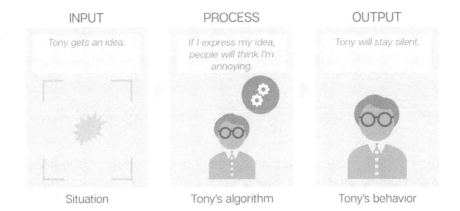

INPUT	PROCESS	OUTPUT
Tony gets an idea.	If I express my idea, people will think I'm annoying.	Tony will stay silent.
Situation	Tony's algorithm	Tony's behavior

Even 25 years later, in a meeting at his job, Tony struggles to speak up about his ideas. He is afraid that people will find his ideas bad and not like him because of it. Tony tells himself, "Don't be annoying and a know-it-all. The idea is probably not as good as you think."

When a seemingly innocent situation is repeated many times in your childhood, it can lead to a harmful outcome many years later.

Paula's spillage

Paula is six years old and takes a cup of tea from the kitchen. She loves tea, because it's warm and tasty. While walking to the living room with a smile, she drops some tea on the floor.

Martina, the babysitter, sees it and breaks out in anger, "Damn! Why are you so careless? The floor was spotless! I just spent hours cleaning and now you've just messed it up again."

Paula feels sad. When similar situations keep happening in the future, Paula creates the following belief:

If I make a little mistake, **then** people will not like me.

To prevent this from happening, she forms the following algorithm:

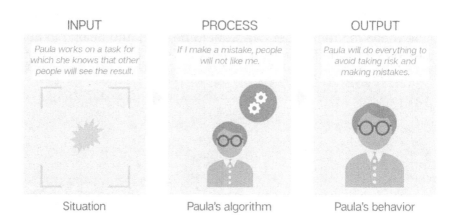

INPUT	PROCESS	OUTPUT
Paula works on a task for which she knows that other people will see the result.	If I make a mistake, people will not like me.	Paula will do everything to avoid taking risk and making mistakes.
Situation	Paula's algorithm	Paula's behavior

Even 30 years later, Paula struggles with her perfectionistic belief while working on a report. She spends 2 and a half hours formatting a table in her Excel spreadsheet, afraid that her boss won't approve of her if it's not perfect.

Eventually, Paula goes to sleep at 3:00 a.m. and feels exhausted the next day. When she gets into the office, Paula sees that her boss didn't even use the table in his presentation. Paula assumes that her boss doesn't find her good enough, leaving her with a feeling of worthlessness.

Even though Paula has good intentions, her action leads to a counterproductive outcome.

Principle #5:

Algorithms that are formed in your childhood can still have a large impact on your behavior today.

CHAPTER 5:
BENEFICIAL ALGORITHMS

The previous examples demonstrate that situations in your childhood can have a negative impact on your behavior today. However, that doesn't mean we haven't built any beneficial algorithms. That's why these beneficial algorithms are the focus of this chapter.

We aren't always aware of the harmful algorithms we have built in our life. These unknown weaknesses are often referred to as "blind spots". On the other hand, we also have strengths that we aren't aware of. Adam Grant, an American professor of psychology, refers to these as "bright spots". One of the reasons why you may be unaware of a certain strength is because the behavior that is appreciated by others seems "normal" to us.

One of the bright spots that I discovered is my ability to create structure in chaos. I discovered this ability in 2016 when my colleagues and I were working on a proposal for a new consulting project. As always with proposals, pressure was high. We had only seven days to present a convincing solution to the client. After four full days of work in a small room, something unfortunate happened.

One expert, who wasn't available before, entered the room with bad news. To our astonishment, he told us that one of our key assumptions was incorrect. As a result, the solution we had worked on was worthless. My colleagues and I looked at each other. Only three days to go. Was this ever going to work? Everyone knew this project was crucial.

Emotions rose. And so did the room temperature. One director said he couldn't believe no one challenged the crucial assumption. I looked at the bags under his eyes, which revealed the late nights of work. Another director elaborated on different scenarios, but no one seemed to understand. Half an hour later, everyone was in a heavy discussion, deep down in the details. We weren't making any progress. Then I took a pen and walked to the whiteboard. I wrote down the new challenge we faced. Slowly, colleagues started to add to the overview I was writing down. As a result, the discussion was more structured.

Writing down the core of the problem was automatic for me. Apparently, I had an algorithm like this:

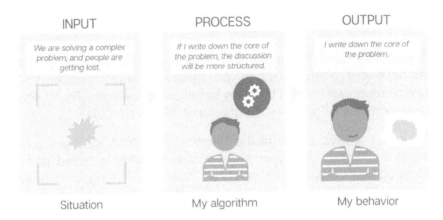

INPUT	PROCESS	OUTPUT
We are solving a complex problem, and people are getting lost.	If I write down the core of the problem, the discussion will be more structured.	I write down the core of the problem.
Situation	My algorithm	My behavior

For me, bringing clarity into chaos is a logical step. It doesn't take much effort from my side. However, later that day, people told me that it was a turning point in our meeting. Having the challenge clearly written down helped us understand the new challenge. As a result, we could come up with solutions to deliver the proposal within the deadline. Later, I received similar positive feedback in other complex situations.

I thought, "I didn't even do anything." For me, breaking down problems comes naturally. While my behavior felt normal to me, this action helped other people significantly. I realized that this was a positive algorithm, something I needed to keep doing. Now that I am aware of this strength, I can also see how it might help in other types of situations.

You too may have strengths that you aren't aware of. When did you receive positive feedback even though you thought your behavior was totally ordinary? In other words, what are your bright spots? As an analytical thinker, maybe you excel at breaking down problems. Maybe you benefit from great curiosity. Or perhaps you always arrive well-prepared to meetings.

Even though it's important to work on harmful algorithms that hinder your growth, I am a strong believer in developing your strengths. In

Part 2, I will give you tips to maximize the positive impact of your beneficial algorithms.

Principle #6:

Next to our harmful algorithms, everyone has built a set of beneficial algorithms. Most people aren't aware of all their beneficial algorithms, because the behavior feels automatic and ordinary. Becoming aware of those positive triggers helps to maximize their impact.

Batman and Joker algorithms

So, you probably understand the concept of beneficial and harmful algorithms. From now on, I will refer to them as *"Batman and Joker algorithms"*. Why? Like your beneficial algorithms, Batman knows the right thing to do. He has the courage to act, even when it's difficult. Batman is strong and has traits that are attractive to other people. When others observe his intelligent behavior, they are inspired to grow and develop similar strengths.

In contrast, harmful algorithms don't serve us at all. Like a harmful algorithm, the Joker is scarred by the past. He is sneaky and manipulative. The Joker tells stories and thereby tricks you into the wrong behavior. He feels no empathy and damages personal relationships. Nobody is inspired by his behavior.

CHAPTER 6:
AWARENESS OF YOUR OWN ALGORITHMS

Do you want an incentive for becoming more aware of your algorithms that you have built in your life? In her book *Insight*, Tasha Eurich demonstrates strong scientific evidence that more self-awareness makes you happier, more successful, more confident, and better at communicating with others. Eurich's research also shows that 90% of people believe they are self-aware, but according to her definition, only 15% of them are.[14] This is an example of the Dunning-Kruger effect: people tend to overestimate their own cognitive ability.[15] In any case, how do you get to be part of this exclusive group of self-aware people?

Three effective ways to better understand your own algorithms are as follows:

1) Ask for feedback

2) Meditate

3) Keep a journal

Ask for feedback

You see the world through your own pair of glasses. That's why we see our behavior with a biased perspective. Strikingly, other people generally see us more objectively than we see ourselves. This is what psychologist Timothy Smith and his colleagues illustrated in research with 300 married couples who were tested for heart disease. In the study, each participant needed to rate both their own and their partner's levels of anger, hostility, and argumentativeness. All these traits are strong predictors of heart disease. The researchers concluded that people's self-ratings were infinitely less accurate than those of their spouses.[16]

Getting the perspective of those around you is important. That is also what I found out in 2015 when I was having lunch with a colleague. I looked at my watch and saw that it was a few minutes before 1:00 p.m. I said goodbye to my colleague because I had an important client meeting.

I was right on time, excited for the session. An hour later, I said goodbye to the client and made my way to the bathroom. While walking down the stairs, I reflected on how the meeting went. "Could have been better, I thought. Well, he seemed happy with the solution I presented, but it didn't feel great. Maybe I can…"

Then, I entered the bathroom and something interrupted my thought. I looked in the mirror. My heartbeat sky-rocketed. WHAT!

A piece of spinach. Right in the middle of my teeth. Did I talk to the client for a whole hour and he didn't tell me about it? And my colleague — he didn't say anything either?

Well, I can blame my colleague and the client for not saying anything. But I won't achieve anything with that. A more powerful thought is, "What could I have done differently?" Next meeting, I could take the time to check my teeth and use a toothpick. Nevertheless, if you see me walking around with a piece of spinach in my teeth, I'd still encourage you to tell me. But that's not the main point of my story.

This story demonstrates that many people find it difficult to tell you what is on their mind. They don't want to make you uncomfortable and are afraid that you'll dislike them. Evolution, remember?

The point is, we all have metaphorical spinach in our teeth. We all have tics and tendencies (that is, algorithms) we aren't aware of. People are unlikely to tell us about these algorithms because they don't want to hurt our feelings. The best you can do is show that it's safe to tell the truth. Open the gate to feedback and tell others you appreciate honesty. Asking for feedback is uncomfortable, but it helps you understand your algorithms and become more confident in social interactions. Your rider knows that asking for feedback is valuable in the long run, but your emotional elephant wants comfort now. Then your rider rationalizes why it's okay not to ask for feedback: "My colleagues are probably too busy to give me feedback." Or "Perhaps my teammate doesn't know me well enough." If you let your emotional elephant win the fight, you eliminate all of your opportunities to grow. Do you choose comfort or courage?

If we don't ask how our teeth look, people may never tell us. We end up messing up important meetings because of something that we could have fixed. And who knows, maybe it's not a piece of spinach in our teeth, but a piece of gold instead. Through feedback, we may not only discover our blind spots; we may find our bright spots too.

When I was a child, I had a great-aunt who always came by on my birthday. I didn't know her well, but she always brought me a present. That was sweet. The thing is, she often gave me a present that wasn't even close to fitting my interests. I didn't understand why you would go birthday shopping for a nine-year-old boy who loves soccer, then come back home with a vase. Every year, I unwrapped the gift paper, knowing that I would not care much about the present. But my parents taught me to say "thank you." Always. When people buy you a present, they invest their time and energy.

The same is true when you receive feedback. You won't always like the message. You won't always understand it. However, that person made an effort to share the gift of feedback with you. The least you can do is thank them.

The keep/start/stop method

A feedback method that works well for me is the keep/start/stop method. It's simple: ask the people you work with the following three questions:

1) What should I keep doing?

2) What should I start doing?

3) What should I stop doing?

Ask them for at least one example situation. That way, you'll start to recognize your algorithms. The answers give you insights that you can directly translate to your algorithms.

Question	Insight from the answer
What should I keep doing?	Suggests which Batman algorithms you have
What should I start doing?	Suggests which new algorithms would be valuable for you to build
What should I stop doing?	Reveals your Joker algorithms

These questions have been more useful to me than a broad question like "Can you give me some feedback?" because people tend to find it difficult to give feedback without any guidelines. I encourage you to discuss the answers face to face, as this leads to a deeper understanding. Try not to defend your behavior. Only listen, ask questions, and take notes.

Keep in mind: even if you feel that the feedback you receive is completely inaccurate, feedback is valuable. At the very least, it will inform you of how other people perceive you.

Exercise #1:

- *Discover some spinach (or gold) on your teeth.*

Before the end of next week, schedule a meeting with a colleague to ask for feedback with the keep/start/stop-method.

I can imagine you will find this challenging. If that's the case, asking for feedback on a specific task can make the step smaller. For example: ask a colleague what he or she has seen from you when you worked on an analysis, did a presentation, or led a client meeting.

Meditate

I remember the first time I heard about meditation. My first thought was "This stuff is too spiritual for me." I am a guy who likes numbers. "Prove to me that it works."

Then, somebody did. I read about scientific studies that demonstrated how meditation changes the brain.

I thought, "Okay, let's give it a try." It was challenging to build the habit. Sitting down still felt counterproductive. Trying to focus on my breath seemed stupid. So many interesting things to do and I was just sitting there...

But after 5 years and more than 1,400 sessions, I meditate almost every day for 10 minutes. Meditation has been one of the main contributors to my growth.

- I have become a better listener.
- I have gained more confidence.
- My concentration has improved.
- My energy levels have increased.

And, importantly, I have become much more aware of my own algorithms. Meditation helps me to assess when my emotional elephant is being lazy and when my elephant has a valuable message to share.

If you don't meditate, I can imagine the idea of meditating feels daunting. Luckily, there are many free applications that can guide you step by step. If you would consider meditating, give them a try.

Keep a journal

Another powerful way to become more aware of your algorithms is by writing a journal. That way, you can analyze the software in your mind: what code is performing well and what parts do you want to reprogram?

As a starting point, reflect on your working day and think "When did my emotion change significantly?" These are the most valuable situations to zoom in on. If you feel a bit annoyed after a meeting, it can be rewarding to analyze what happened.

For example:

1) Did this senior colleague interrupt you when you shared your idea?

2) Did the dominant team member make an insensitive remark about your presentation?

3) Did that business guy impatiently jump to the next topic when you were explaining important technical details?

Let's assume the first situation happened. To dive deeper and see the results, we can do a *behavior–impact analysis*:

Behavior-impact analysis: example	
Situation What happened?	When I proposed my idea, a senior guy interrupted and changed the topic.
Behavior What did I do?	I stayed silent the rest of the meeting.
Rational impact What was the result?	Nobody understood my idea.
Emotional impact How I did I feel?	I felt unappreciated.

This suggests that I have an algorithm that looks like:

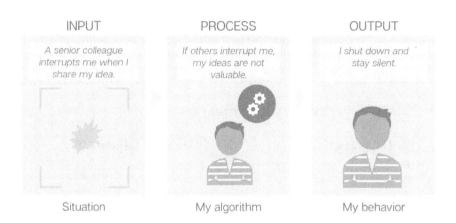

INPUT	PROCESS	OUTPUT
A senior colleague interrupts me when I share my idea.	If others interrupt me, my ideas are not valuable.	I shut down and stay silent.
Situation	My algorithm	My behavior

This analysis is valuable in two ways:

1) You find out how your algorithm works

2) You see the impact of your algorithm. It helps to analyze whether your behavior leads to the desired results.

If your behavior doesn't lead to your desired results, this analysis can help you identify how you could optimize your algorithm. You could ask yourself "What can I do differently next time to obtain positive results?" We'll look at such questions in the next chapter.

Principle #7:

Feedback, meditation, and journaling can help you become more aware of your algorithms.

Write down your algorithms

Exercise #2:

- *Write down your algorithms.*

You've seen several examples from childhood and professional life. Did this trigger any thoughts about your own behavior? What have people said about your behavior in the past? Which situations did your emotions significantly change in?

With the examples from the last chapters in mind, write down a few of your algorithms. Write down at least one Batman algorithm and one Joker algorithm.

Batman algorithms: your strengths

INPUT (situation)   **OUTPUT (your behavior)**
IF: ....   THEN: ....

INPUT (situation)   **OUTPUT (your behavior)**
IF: ....   THEN: ....

Joker algorithms: your weaknesses

INPUT (situation)   **OUTPUT (your behavior)**
IF: ....   THEN: ....

INPUT (situation)   **OUTPUT (your behavior)**
IF: ....   THEN: ....

Done?

Great!

If you haven't done it yet, take the time to write down your algorithms now. Reading about human behavior won't change anything in your interactions with others. Only if you're willing to take action will you be able to increase your social confidence, build joyful relationships, and persuade others with conviction.

CONCLUSION PART 1

You can see your brain as a set of algorithms. All situational variables are taken as input and processed into an output. Next to factual variables, emotional variables are always part of your algorithms. Therefore, the better you understand what makes your emotions go up and down, the better you understand your algorithms. And the better you understand your algorithms, the easier the interactions with other people become. You become powerful when you can tap into both your rational brain and your emotional brain. Embrace emotions and use them to your advantage; that's how you increase your emotional intelligence.

A better understanding of your algorithms is crucial in your interactions with other people. If your algorithms are black boxes, you have no clue what happens. You just respond to situations in front of you, without any awareness. You have no control nor influence. You can become more aware of your algorithms by asking for feedback, meditating, or writing in a journal.

Understanding your own algorithms is a huge step forward in getting the results you want in your professional and personal life. However, this is only where your journey starts.

- This book proceeds with Part 2: Optimize. Through a combination of theory and practice, you'll learn how to reprogram your mind: change your Joker algorithms and get the most out of your Batman algorithms.

- Then, Part 3 focuses on understanding the algorithms of others. This understanding will help you tremendously. You will know what other people find important and how they will behave. No more small talk you don't enjoy. Instead, you'll be able to build deep and fulfilling relationships with the people around you. Imagine walking into a room with confidence because you know that your interactions will be easy and fun.

- Lastly, Part 4 explains the three steps to increase your influence. By avoiding the single mistake that almost everyone makes, you'll be able to become a master at persuasion.

PART 2

OPTIMIZE: CHANGE YOUR BEHAVIOR

INTRODUCTION

In Part 1, we examined how your algorithms are formed and how you can become more self-aware. Now it's time to analyze what results you achieve through your algorithms and how you can optimize them. We optimize our algorithms by changing our behavior, as you'll see.

OUTPUT

My behavior

The more often you follow a pattern, the stronger an algorithm becomes. That's why older algorithms tend to be more powerful: after a pattern repeats many times, it's ingrained in your mind. This results in the same behavior over and over again. It works almost effortlessly — and often unconsciously. Psychologists always ask for your childhood and family situation because they want to understand what beliefs and patterns you've formed in the past. Some of those algorithms are now running your life — for the better or worse.

This doesn't mean that you can't change anything though — you can! The process is simple, but it's not easy. That's why I'll guide you, step by step, with a clear example. Again, I will only provide the tools. It's up to you what you do with it. Taking action is the only way to improve your people skills.

CHAPTER 7: EVALUATE YOUR ALGORITHMS: BEHAVIOR-IMPACT ANALYSIS

To decide what algorithms you want to optimize, analyze the results of your algorithms. You can do that with the *behavior–impact analysis* introduced in Part 1. We will use this method for both the Joker and Batman algorithms.

Principle #8:

The behavior–impact analysis helps you understand the results of your Batman and Joker algorithms. The results suggest what algorithms you should optimize.

Impact of Joker algorithms

Exercise #3:

■ *Write down the impact of your Joker algorithm.*

Instructions:

1) *Pick one of the Joker algorithms you wrote down in Part 1.*

2) *Think about a situation at work in which you used this algorithm, and write the results down in the following table.*

My algorithm of saying no is given as an example.

	Saying no (my example)	Your algorithm (for you to fill in)
Situation What was the trigger?	My colleague asked me for help while I was busy.	....
Behavior What did I do?	I said "I think I can do it."	....
Rational impact What was the result?	I didn't spend as much time on my own responsibilities as I had planned.	....
Emotional impact How did I feel?	I felt stressed. I was disappointed with the results of my work. I felt angry with myself for not being clear. And I felt a bit annoyed with the person who asked for help.	....

Impact of Batman algorithms

Exercise #4:

■ *Write down the impact of your **Batman** algorithm.*

Instructions:

1) *Pick one of your Batman algorithms you wrote down in Part 1.*

2) *Think about a situation at work in which you used this algorithm, and write the results down in the table below.*

My algorithm of "structure in chaos" is given as an example

	Structure in chaos (my example)	Your algorithm (for you to fill in)
Situation	While solving a problem, we got lost in a detailed and unstructured discussion.	....
Behavior What did I do?	I summarized the core problem and wrote it down.	....
Rational impact What was the result?	We made a big step toward solving the problem.	....
Emotional impact How I did I feel?	I felt happy, energetic, and motivated.	....

The results of your algorithms: a recipe for change

Of course, your algorithms don't always lead to the same impact in each situation. However, when you do this exercise on a regular basis (e.g. every week), you will soon be able to observe a pattern.

Do you remember what you had for dinner yesterday? You probably do. What about ten days ago? Difficult, right? Remembering emotions is usually even harder. Most people aren't able to accurately describe how they felt one day ago, let alone give a precise description of their emotions two weeks back. That's why I advise you to minimize the time between the situation and the moment of writing down the impact. Ideally, write down the impact immediately after the situation occurred. Alternatively, build a new habit and write down one behavior–impact analysis every night before you go to sleep.

Now look at the results of your algorithms. What results do they produce? If they continually lead to undesirable results (whether rational or emotional), you have a beautiful recipe for change. To tell you more about the ingredients and to explain how you can slow-cook your Joker algorithms until the nastiest bacteria have died, let's go back to my example algorithm of saying no. Because of this algorithm, I didn't spend enough time on my own responsibilities. Moreover, I felt stressed and disappointed.

Is that something I want to change?

Oh, yes.

CHAPTER 8:
CHANGE YOUR JOKER ALGORITHMS

Most behavior is automatic, and that's good. Otherwise, we would spend most of our time awake thinking about the best response to a specific situation. Luckily, we don't need to think about taking a shower or stopping for a traffic light. That would lead to many (smelly) accidents.

For algorithms that we want to change, however, we need a conscious approach. And the approach may surprise you.

Instead of trying to modify our algorithms directly, we are going to change the output. That is, we change our behavior.

INPUT   PROCESS   OUTPUT

My behavior

Why this seemingly indirect method? As psychologist Timothy Wilson explains in his book *Strangers to Ourselves*, "One of the most enduring lessons of social psychology is that behavior change often precedes changes in attitudes and feelings."[17]

In other words: change in behavior first. Change in algorithms second.

How come? The reason lies in cognitive dissonance. Cognitive dissonance is a situation in which our beliefs (how we think we should behave) conflict with our actions (how we do behave). Our brain hates these kind of situations. That's why our brains rationalize our new behavior and tell us that it must be in line with our beliefs.

To give you a quick example, imagine you're working from home. Although you have an important task to work on, you find yourself reading the news. Your belief (I should be productive) conflicts with your action (I'm not productive). But then you realize that you read an article about workplace productivity, which emphasized the importance of taking breaks. That's why you tell yourself "I'm just increasing my productivity."

If you remember the example from chapter 2, this is the rider speaking, finding a logical justification for the impulsive action of the emotional elephant. The rider takes away your guilty sensation for not being productive. Feels great, does it not?

In this example, cognitive dissonance does not contribute to your productivity.

However, there is a way to make cognitive dissonance work in your favor.

When you choose a desirable behavior, your brain will tell you that this is indeed the best choice. Repeating this behavior over and over makes your beliefs (and thus, algorithms) adjust too. As a result, you don't have to consciously think about choosing a new behavior. The new behavior is automatically chosen by your new algorithm.

Your algorithms are like a highway; you have taken that route every time in your life because the highway is fast and easy. Your new algorithm is a hidden path through the undergrowth where you have to cut down bushes along the way. If you keep forcing yourself up the hidden path, it eventually becomes the highway. The old highway gets overgrown and forgotten about.

Changing your algorithms step by step

Here we are. In the previous chapter, you chose one Joker algorithm that you want to change. Ready for optimization?

Let's go back in time. I was working on a project for a large Dutch bank as a data analyst. My responsibility was to find customer insights in e-commerce data. For example, predicting what website visitors were interested in. This prediction helped marketeers to personalize the website content for each visitor.

This particular day, one of the marketeers passed by my desk. He wanted to get a better understanding of the people who visited the credit card pages. As soon as my colleague asked for help, my algorithm turned on, grabbed the input, and spit out my behavior. The instant response was my emotional elephant speaking. He didn't enjoy planning and looking into the future. My elephant wants to relax instead of going through the pain of setting clear expectations with the person asking for my help. Easier to take away the social tension and not upset the other person. Before I realized it, I said yes.

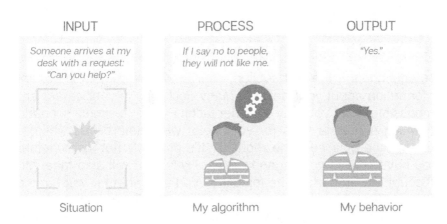

INPUT	PROCESS	OUTPUT
Someone arrives at my desk with a request: "Can you help?"	If I say no to people, they will not like me.	"Yes."
Situation	My algorithm	My behavior

In the last section, we saw that this automatic response didn't give me the desired results. The focus of my elephant on short-term comfort led to issues in the longer term. But how do we change this?

Well, we can change our Joker algorithms in three steps:

1) Catch yourself. Pause.

2) Experiment with different behavior.

3) Repeat and monitor the results.

Step 1: Catch yourself. Pause.

The first step is to catch yourself by recognizing that this is a situation that triggered your Joker algorithm in the past. This step is crucial because when you let your algorithm respond automatically, it's likely that you'll get the same negative results. In my example: no clear expectations, less time for my own work, and disappointment.

For algorithms that you have followed many times, your behavior is so automatic that it's difficult to catch yourself. This will be easier the more self-aware you become.

When you recognize the situation, stop. Don't move; keep your mouth shut. Try to breath slowly and deliberately for at least three cycles of inhalation and exhalation.

Instead of giving an auto-response, ask yourself "How do I *feel*?"

Being an analytical person who used to disregard feelings, I found this a daunting task. I thought, "What do you mean, how do I feel? I don't know. I guess I don't feel much."

As described in the last section, your emotions contain important information about your desires. Many decisions in your career are impossible when you only consider facts. Even in a simple scenario in which someone asks for your help, what determines whether you decline or accept the request? It's probably not just whether you have time in your agenda. Most likely, you will also take into account how important the topic is to you and whether you have a good relationship with the person asking. These two variables are difficult to quantify. That's why it's valuable to become more aware of your emotional elephant.

Do you feel bothered by the request because this is a topic you don't care about?

Or do you feel energetic to help because it's a topic you want to learn about?

Do you feel a tension in your stomach because you have a date night scheduled and you don't want to disappoint your partner by being late? Or is there a feeling of excitement because helping this person leads to more learning opportunities for you?

When you take the time to ask yourself such questions, you train yourself to read your emotions. In this process, it can help to observe the physical sensations in your body. Over time, you learn to recognize which kind of physical discomfort comes with each type of emotion. Slowly, you will get better at reading your feelings. "Is this my emotional elephant pushing for short-term comfort? Or is it trying to tell me something valuable this time?"

In decision-making, outlining the rational pros and cons was never an issue for me. My problem was that I completely disregarded the emotional side. When I started giving my feelings more attention, I got a more accurate view of the emotional variables. Since I had a more complete picture with both rational and emotional variables, I could make an optimal decision. Namely, saying no when I felt in my stomach that committing to helping the other person didn't feel good.

Thus, the pause achieves three important things:

1) The pause gives you time to look at the complete situation, involving both your rational and emotional brain. In my example, the pause helps to remember that saying yes to one thing means saying no to something else.

2) The pause helps you connect with your feelings. Remember, every now and then your emotional elephant tells you something important. In my case, the pause helped me understand how I feel about this request for help.

3) The pause breaks your pattern and gives you time to implement a new type of behavior. This pause may feel uncomfortable at first. Why is the silence so uncomfortable? Again, blame evolution. We want to belong to our tribe and not upset the people around us. Often, we think that others expect us to respond to a question immediately. But, is this not a story we're telling ourselves? It's not weird to pause. In contrast, it's in the interests of the other person to come up with a thoughtful response.

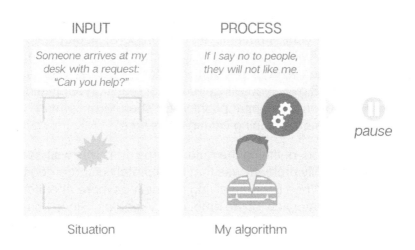

INPUT

Someone arrives at my desk with a request: "Can you help?"

PROCESS

If I say no to people, they will not like me.

pause

Situation

My algorithm

Step 2: Experiment with different behavior

Now that you've broken your old pattern, it's time to build a new one.

In this step, you choose a different type of behavior. Adopting a new behavior is difficult because your emotional elephant is strong and wants to go for the path you've always followed. That's why it can help to think about this step before the situation unfolds.

I screwed up many times, saying yes even though it wasn't what I wanted. And that's okay. I try to learn step by step. Adopting a new behavior is always the hardest in the beginning. According to Philippa Lally, a health psychology researcher, on average it takes 66 days to build a new habit. However, the number of days you need until a habit is ingrained highly depends on the situation.[18] One of the influencing factors is how often you practice your new behavior. This change requires persistence, but the results are rewarding.

Remember that you have the power to correct yourself if you find yourself falling into your old pattern. In the case of my example, "Hey, I said that I could help you, but now I see I don't have the time. I'm sorry." Of course, it's easier to say that you don't have the time before you commit to helping. That's why it pays to catch yourself before your algorithms trick you into saying yes.

The pause from step 1 gives you more time to implement a new behavior. Despite this extra time, it's hard to understand the complete picture of rational and (especially) emotional variables in the moment itself. That's why it can help to ask whether you can get back to the other person later. This extends the pause and buys you time to find out what you really want. The benefit is that you aren't pressured by the other person (that is, pressured by your own algorithm) into saying yes. Note that this isn't only a benefit for you. Setting clear expectations is useful for the other person too.

INPUT	PROCESS	OUTPUT
Someone arrives at my desk with a request: "Can you help?"	If I say no to people, they will not like me.	"I want to check if this fits my schedule. Can I get back to you?"
		pause
Situation	My algorithm	My behavior

Step 3: Repeat and monitor the results

After implementing a new type of behavior, you see that the new behavior leads to positive results.

In the example of saying no:

- **Rational impact:**
  - ☐ I have more time for projects and tasks that are important to me.
  - ☐ I set clear expectations with others. It's clear to others what I will and won't do.
- **Emotional impact:**
  - ☐ I feel more confident, more in control, and less stressed.

The results are a mental reward, a little candy for your emotional elephant. Your emotional brain loves it and will try to get the candy again next time. That's how a new algorithm is formed.

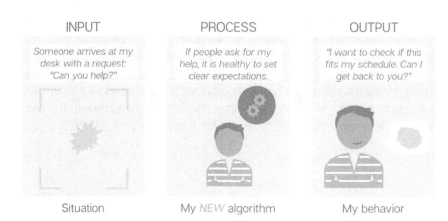

INPUT	PROCESS	OUTPUT
Someone arrives at my desk with a request: "Can you help?"	If people ask for my help, it is healthy to set clear expectations.	"I want to check if this fits my schedule. Can I get back to you?"
Situation	My NEW algorithm	My behavior

Now, if someone asks me to help, I don't instantly respond by saying yes. Sometimes I buy myself extra time. Sometimes I say no. And sometimes I still say yes in the moment. However, if I do, it's a deliberate choice instead of a blind auto-response. My increased awareness of what's going on inside me helps me make better decisions.

By monitoring the results, I see that the outcome is not as bad as my emotional brain expects. If I say no, this doesn't always mean that people are angry and dislike me. Usually, they understand. Seeing those results makes it easier to say no the next time, and this initiates a beautiful snowball effect. Journaling can help to make these small steps of progress visible.

Paula and Tony

Do you remember Paula's spillage and Tony's beautiful train track? They could apply these same three steps to their Joker algorithms: pause, new behavior, repeat.

What would that look like?

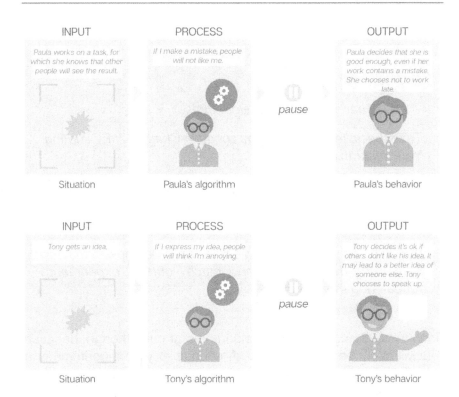

INPUT	PROCESS	OUTPUT
Paula works on a task, for which she knows that other people will see the result.	If I make a mistake, people will not like me. *pause*	Paula decides that she is good enough, even if her work contains a mistake. She chooses not to work late.
Situation	Paula's algorithm	Paula's behavior

INPUT	PROCESS	OUTPUT
Tony gets an idea.	If I express my idea, people will think I'm annoying. *pause*	Tony decides it's ok if others don't like his idea. It may lead to a better idea of someone else. Tony chooses to speak up.
Situation	Tony's algorithm	Tony's behavior

Through these conscious actions, Paula and Tony ensure that their emotional elephant doesn't take over the show. Making changes to these deeply ingrained Joker algorithms isn't easy. However, by repeating this process over and over, they can implement the more desirable behavior and build Batman algorithms.

Principle #9:

Through a 3-step method (catch yourself, experiment, repeat) you can develop new behavior. As a result, your algorithms change too.

Now it's up to you!

> ***Exercise #5:***
>
> ■ *Change your Joker algorithms.*
>
> *Take the Joker algorithm you chose in Chapter 7: Evaluating Your Algorithms.*
>
> *Now think what behavior you could implement. What could you say or do that will lead to the results you want?*
>
> *Write it down and put it into action!*
>
> *Get into the social jungle and try out your new behavior by walking through the steps: catch yourself, experiment, repeat, and monitor the results.*

Don't try to change all of your algorithms at once though, because you will likely be overwhelmed. A change in your algorithms is a behavior change, similar to building new habits. Starting a new workout routine is doable. But if you want to implement a workout routine, improve your diet, and start meditation all at the same time, you are unlikely to succeed.

Also, it's worth noting that changing your algorithms is not a one-time exercise. Your environment changes; that's why I suggest you have a deeper look at your algorithms at least once a year. Take a rainy Sunday afternoon to look at yourself. Perform a behavior–impact analysis, write down your algorithms, and ask for feedback from the people around you.

What changes do you want to make to your algorithms? It's easy to fall back into old patterns or create new unhealthy ones. By regularly analyzing your algorithms, you keep your software up to date and ensure you are prepared for the best performance.

In this chapter, we started to change our Joker algorithms. Another way to get better results is to maximize the value from our Batman algorithms. We'll do that next.

CHAPTER 9:
MAXIMIZE THE VALUE
OF YOUR BATMAN
ALGORITHMS

In contrast to our Joker algorithms, there is no need to change our Batman algorithms. They already produce the desirable behavior. So, is there a way to get even more out of our Batman algorithms?

Yes, there is. But first, we need to change our focus from the output of our algorithms (our behavior) to the input of our algorithms (the situation).

INPUT

PROCESS

OUTPUT

Situation

Your algorithm

Your behavior

Find your Batman opportunities

As mentioned, you have some Batman algorithms that help you produce positive results. Now, your job is to find more situations where you can apply those algorithms. Basically, you find inputs for your Batman algorithms: situations where you can make use of your strengths.

Do you remember my example algorithm "structure in chaos"? Since I'm aware of this algorithm, I can now try to apply it in similar situations.

You can optimize your Batman algorithms in three steps:

1) Recognize a situation where you can apply your Batman algorithm and find the input.

2) Apply your algorithm.

3) Repeat and monitor the results.

Example:

1) I try to recognize a problem-solving situation where people are lost.

2) I summarize the core of the problem and write it down on a whiteboard.

3) I repeat and analyze: what worked and what didn't?

When I keep doing this, I become a master at recognizing situations that call for my strengths. At some point, I don't think about it anymore. I get good at finding situations that ask for my strengths. My algorithm automatically triggers the behavior that leads to the positive results.

Principle #10:

When you can recognize situations where you can apply your Batman algorithms, you get the most out of your strengths.

Exercise #6:

■ *Optimize your Batman algorithms.*

Take the Batman algorithm you chose in Chapter 7: Evaluating Your Algorithms. Now ask yourself what opportunities you've had in the past to use this Batman algorithm. Have you missed any opportunities?

Then, reflect on how you can apply this algorithm in more situations in the future.

CHAPTER 10:
CREATE THE OPTIMAL
ENVIRONMENT FOR
YOUR ALGORITHMS

We all have a certain environment that works best for us. What environment makes you thrive? Do you work best in silence or with music in the background? Do you prefer to work together for most of the day or on your own? Are you more productive at home or in the office? And at which time of day?

Your environment is a constant input to your algorithms. The question is: what do you do with this input?

You have three main options:

1) Complain

2) Accept

3) Change

Some people choose the first option. Again, that's our emotional elephant speaking, choosing the easiest path. If we blame external factors, we don't seem to bear any responsibility. It feels relaxing. Our elephant feels better after pushing away the responsibility. The second alternative is to accept the situation as it is. While that's better than wasting your energy and spreading energy through your complaints, there are often possibilities to improve the situation. However, changing the situation will require effort from your side. You need to use your rational brain — the rider — to steer the elephant in the right direction. Through a conscious approach, you can choose the more difficult — but more rewarding — path.

Imagine the following example. Conrad has a lot of meetings at work. As a result, he finds it difficult to get work done. Some of

Conrad's Joker algorithms are triggered. He complains to his colleagues during lunch and gossips about the person who sets up many meetings. "Why does he not see that these meetings are ineffective?" Another colleague agrees, "Way too many meetings indeed. Also, I'm getting so tired of all the emails."

Michael, the third person at the lunch table, doesn't say much. He agrees with the points of his colleagues but has a different way of thinking. Instead of complaining, Michael asks a powerful question, "What can we do to improve the situation?"

Soon, this question leads to some new questions and ideas:

- We could inform the guy who sets up many meetings through an automated report.
- Can we do the meetings standing up? This may shorten the time we spend in meetings.
- We could save time in other ways. For example, by reducing the amount of time we spend on emails. Can we use a different medium?

In any negative situation you find yourself in, you can go from *complain* to *change* by asking yourself "What can *I* do to improve the situation?"

That is exactly the question I asked myself.

Thanks to journaling, I discovered two insights:

1) I am most concentrated and productive in the morning
2) On days with a lot of meetings in the morning, I felt a bit annoyed and frustrated

I felt tempted to *complain*. Then I realized it would be better to switch to *change*.

What can *I* do?

I started blocking the first two hours of each day in my agenda to work on the most important tasks. When people requested a meeting in the morning, I tried to plan it in the afternoon. Moreover, I strived to minimize distractions in the morning as much as possible.

The result:

- **Rational impact:** I got much more work done
- **Emotional impact:** I felt energetic, with a sense of progress and fulfillment

I could complain about other people for distracting me and planning those morning meetings. But how can I blame them if they don't know my preferences? That's why I now proactively tell others that I am most focused in the morning.

Your environment determines the input of your algorithms. However, that doesn't mean you are a victim of your environment.

Principle #11:

Find ways to create your optimal environment. Don't blame others. Instead, analyze what you can do to create your own high-performing environment and act accordingly.

CONCLUSION PART 2

Some of the algorithms that you have built in your life are deeply ingrained in your mind. However, that doesn't mean you can't change anything. Through the behavior-impact analysis, you can examine the results of your behavior. If you are unhappy with what you see, it's time for change.

In three steps (catch yourself, experiment, repeat), you can slowly develop behavior that leads to more productive results. This way, you can counter the tricks that your Joker algorithms play on you.

When you're aware of your Batman algorithms, you can search for opportunities to use them. The better you know how you can apply your Batman algorithms, the more value you will get out of your strengths.

Lastly, as your surroundings determine the input of your algorithms, find ways to create a high-performing environment in which you thrive.

Are you reading this book quickly? Remember that the goal is not to finish the book as fast as you can. The goal is to gain a deep understanding of your own and other people's behavior. Every now and then, put the book down and reflect on your own life. Write down a behavior–impact analysis. Do one of the exercises. Try out a new type of behavior.

Improving your people skills is hard work and a never-ending process. Shortcuts don't exist. Only if you are willing to put in the effort and get out of your comfort zone will you make a lasting impact. I guarantee you, it's worth it.

PART 3

INTERACT: UNDERSTAND OTHER PEOPLE'S ALGORITHMS

INTRODUCTION

In Part 1, we discussed how to understand your own algorithms. Then, in Part 2, we looked at how you can upgrade your own algorithms.

In the first two parts, we mostly looked at general situations as inputs to our algorithms. We did this to keep things simple. However, in this interconnected world, you are only one piece of the puzzle. Your algorithms are often triggered by the behavior of another person. And the other person's algorithms are triggered by your behavior. To better understand these social dynamics, from now on, we will take a specific behavior as an input instead of a general situation. This means we have two main scenarios:

Firstly, your behavior can be the input to other people's algorithms:

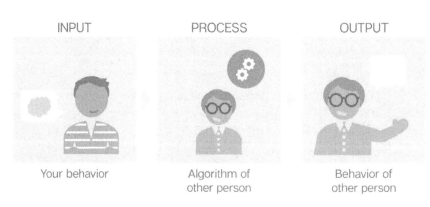

INPUT	PROCESS	OUTPUT
Your behavior	Algorithm of other person	Behavior of other person

Secondly, the other person's behavior can be the input to your algorithm:

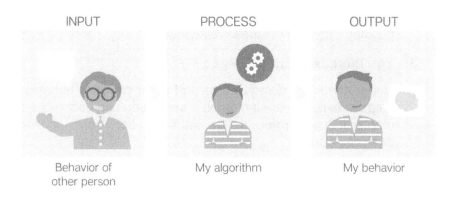

INPUT — Behavior of other person

PROCESS — My algorithm

OUTPUT — My behavior

Keeping these two scenarios in mind, Part 3 discusses how you can better understand other people's algorithms:

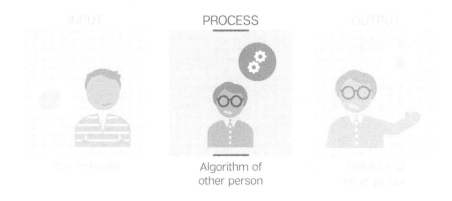

PROCESS — Algorithm of other person

Getting to understand the algorithms of other people has three benefits:

1) **You create better interactions**

The more you know about other people's algorithms, the better you will understand the impact of your behavior on others. Interactions with people you know will usually go smoother. This is true even for interactions with people who have the strangest quirks, because you're aware of their algorithms. Don't we all have that friend? You may even appreciate their oddities.

2) **You build relationships**

When you ask about other people's algorithms, you can show that you're genuinely interested. This attitude of interest can help build to trust, which is a crucial element in building effective business relationships.[19]

3) **You increase your influence**

Understanding the motives behind other people's behavior helps to expand your influence. Finally, you can become the master influencer you always wanted to be. *"Dance for me puppets, dance!"*

Well, not really.

This book does teach you how to increase your influence. However, if your goal is dishonesty and manipulation, you aren't in the right place. The methods in this book will help you expand your positive influence with a focus on transparency and mutual gains. By doing so, you'll be able to influence others while building strong relationships.

CHAPTER 11:
A DEEP DIVE UNDER
THE ICEBERG

Did you know that only 10% of an iceberg is above the water's surface? You can't see the remaining 90% from above the water. This is similar in our daily interactions with others, where we only see what's happening on the surface, namely the other person's behavior. We don't see what is below the surface: everything that is happening in their head and body. And that's a shame, because it's where we find the driving force of the behavior — the algorithms.

To get a better understanding of the driving force behind people's behavior, we need to look under the water. Bring your goggles and don't forget your winter wetsuit. The water is freezing cold. That's why some people only engage in small talk; they find deeper conversations about needs and beliefs uncomfortable.

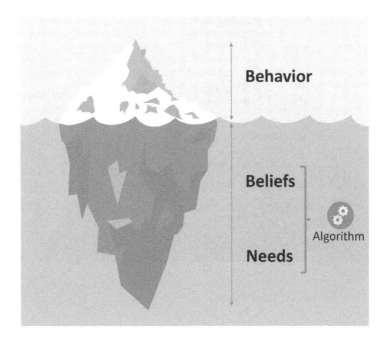

Looking under the water, we see that our algorithms consist of:

- **Needs:** what we want
- **Beliefs:** how we think we should behave to get our needs met

We will look at both elements one by one.

Needs

According to Abraham Maslow, who is among the top ten most-cited psychologists in the 20th century, people are motivated by five basic categories of needs: physiological, safety, belonging and love, esteem, and self-actualization. Combined, these categories form Maslow's hierarchy of needs.[20]

Our most basic needs at the bottom help us to survive. The needs at the top are more abstract.

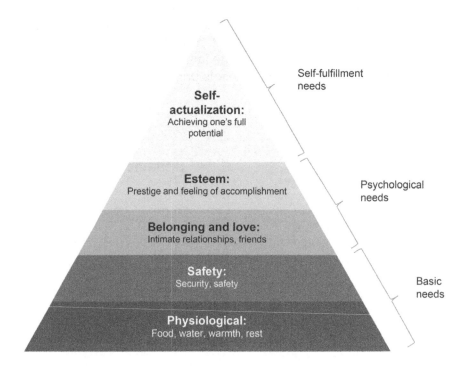

When you have access to this book, your basic needs are most likely fulfilled. In social interactions at work, people are mostly focused on the top three needs of Maslow's hierarchy. To understand these needs a bit better, how do they apply to situations in your job?

1) **Need of belonging**

   Fulfilling relationships with the people at work, a connection with others. The feeling of being part of a group, whether that's on your team, in your department, or in the company as a whole.

2) **Need of esteem**

   Recognition for your accomplishments. A feeling of "I matter."

3) **Need of self-actualization**

   Achieving your full personal potential. Becoming the most you can be.

Beliefs

Your algorithms are based on the belief "If I do X, then my need will be met." You learned in the past that a certain behavior was effective in getting your need met. That's how you formed a new belief.

Remember my Batman algorithm "structure in chaos"? When I'm in a meeting where we get stuck in a complex discussion, I write down the core of the problem and break it down into smaller pieces.

What is my **belief** driving this behavior?

> **If** I write down the problem, **then** the discussion gets more structured and we can reach a solution quicker.

How did I get this belief? I have tried this behavior in the past and I saw it worked, as we reached a solution quicker. People were happy and gave positive feedback. I felt that my contribution mattered thanks to this little accomplishment. Thus, my need for esteem was fulfilled. For this reason, I formed an algorithm and repeated the behavior.

The people skills formula: need–belief–behavior

We can describe algorithms with the people skills formula:

- Person wants to get **[NEED]**.
- Person thinks **[BELIEF]**.
- That is why person does **[BEHAVIOR]**.

For example:

- **Need:** I want to have a sense of contribution to the team and feel recognized.
- **Belief:** I think that writing down the problem will be appreciated by the team and will help solve the problem quicker.
- **Behavior:** That's why I write down the problem.

As you can see in the next illustration, based on beliefs and needs, your algorithms determine the output: behavior.

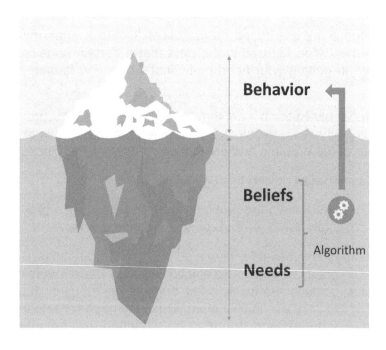

Principle #12:

We can describe algorithms with the people skills formula:

- *Person wants to get [NEED].*
- *Person thinks [BELIEF].*
- *That is why person does [BEHAVIOR].*

CHAPTER 12: MY TALKATIVE COLLEAGUE

We'll dive into the algorithms of other people by going back to 2015. My colleague, let's call her Talisa, starts talking to me about her weekend. It's not a good time to talk, because I'm working to meet a deadline. However, 5 minutes pass and she keeps on talking. I haven't done anything yet, apart from listen. Do you remember my Joker algorithm that made it difficult for me to say no? This scenario is similar because my belief was that saying no (interrupting others or rejecting someone in any other way) would make the person not like me.

- **Need:** Belonging
- **Belief: If** I interrupt Talisa, **then** Talisa will not like me, and I won't have a feeling of belonging.

According to my belief, the result (no feeling of belonging) is the opposite of my need (belonging). That's why I avoid expressing my thoughts ("I don't have time"). Instead, I decide to give her a hint and look out of the window. You can see my belief in the next image under "Process."

INPUT	PROCESS	OUTPUT
Talisa talks to me when I am busy.	If I say no to people, they will not like me.	I look out of the window.

Other person's behavior	My algorithm	My behavior

As you can see, Talisa's behavior is a trigger for my behavior. The opposite is also true. My behavior is an input to Talisa's algorithms. I decide to look distracted, hoping that Talisa will pick up the cue and stop talking. My algorithm determines that "look out the window" is the optimal output. That way, I don't need to say no and I may still reach my goal. I cross my fingers under the table in the hope that she understands my hint.

To my astonishment, she talks even more!

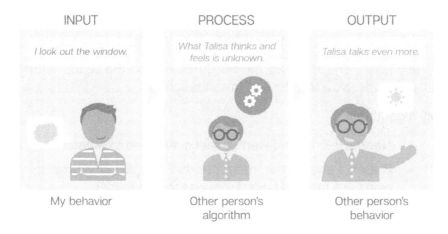

INPUT	PROCESS	OUTPUT
I look out the window.	*What Talisa thinks and feels is unknown.*	*Talisa talks even more.*
My behavior	Other person's algorithm	Other person's behavior

I wanted Talisa to stop talking, but I got the opposite result. To understand why this happened, we need to dive a bit deeper into Talisa's algorithms.

Looking at Maslow's hierarchy of needs, what could be the reason for Talisa talking even more?

A few possibilities are:

- Talisa assumed I didn't feel connected to her:

  ☐ **Need:** Belonging

  ☐ **Belief: If** I talk more, **then** I will become more connected with Gilbert

- Talisa assumed I was distracted and talking more would get my attention:

  ☐ **Need:** Belonging

  ☐ **Belief: If** I talk more, **then** I will get Gilbert's attention

- Talisa assumed I disrespected her. By talking more, she tried to win my approval:

  ☐ **Need:** Esteem

  ☐ **Belief: If** I talk more, **then** I will win Gilbert's approval

- Talisa assumed I wasn't comfortable making direct eye contact. Or she thought that I looked out the window because that helped me reflect on what she said:

  ☐ **Need:** Belonging

  ☐ **Belief: If** I talk keep talking, **then** Gilbert will keep listening and we will keep this fun conversation going

In any case, she misread my social cues and made the wrong assumptions. Now let's look at my situation.

My algorithm is:

- **Need:** Belonging. I want to feel connected to others.
- **Belief:** I should not interrupt other people; otherwise they won't like me and I won't feel connected to them.

Based on my need and my belief, I choose my behavior: I try to give Talisa a subtle hint by looking out the window. I avoid interrupting her, because I think that will lead to disconnection.

Talisa thinks that by talking more, she will fulfil her need for belonging or esteem. However, it turns out that this is *not* an effective strategy. Both Talisa and I are in a situation that neither of us enjoy. In the worst case, Talisa starts talking more, I act more distracted, Talisa starts talking even more, and before I know it, we are in a painful vicious cycle.

I blame Talisa for not picking up on my obvious cues, thinking "Talisa is so self-centered. How can she not see that I want to stop the conversation? I wonder how her partner is able to deal with her." I am making assumptions and paying attention to the destructive thoughts in my head.

Talisa may then blame me for not paying attention, thinking "How can you be so disrespectful, looking out of the window and not listening? This is so anti-social."

I don't feel understood. Talisa doesn't feel understood. Both of us feel frustrated. How do I get out of this situation? By taking responsibility. By considering what I can do to improve the situation.

Principle #13:

Do not blame the other person. Think "What can I do to improve the situation?"

Easy on paper, difficult in practice.

If Talisa starts talking and doesn't stop, what can I do? I could let her talk because I think it's impolite to interrupt people. However, will Talisa really think I'm polite if I look out the window, leaving her feeling ignored?

Based on my (false) belief, I avoid interrupting Talisa. The alternative would be to have a critical look at my belief and understand that Talisa will not dislike me if I tell her it isn't a good time to talk. And maybe it would even be in Talisa's best interests if I expressed my thoughts instead of looking out the window.

So, next time I was busy and she came by to talk, I decided to take a different approach. I had to pause before my auto-response made me listen, keep quiet, then look out of the window.

When Talisa passed by my desk to talk about her weekend, I said, "Talisa, now is not a good time for me to talk. Can we speak later?"

"Yes, that sounds good. Actually, I'm a bit stressed about a deadline I have. I'd like to get your thoughts during lunch," she said.

My deadline was at 11:00 a.m., so meeting at lunch sounded good. That's what we agreed, and Talisa walked over to her desk. I felt relieved.

What did I do differently this time? I considered two points:

1) What is my own need, and how can I tell Talisa about my need? I realized the effect of my behavior on Talisa. I understood that expressing my own need would help her. Not expressing my thoughts leads to assumptions and blame.

2) What is below the surface of Talisa's behavior? In other words, what is her need? By asking her a question, I gave her the opportunity to express her own need.

In doing so, I could make an adjustment to my behavior. Instead of looking bored, hoping she would pick up the vague hint, I took responsibility and honestly expressed what was in my head.

A few weeks later, I had a conversation with Talisa, and what she said blew me away. I told her I find it difficult to interrupt people. She said, "Why? I like it when people do that! It gives me some time to think about what I want to say. And it helps me understand what's going on in the other person's head."

Wow. I never expected that.

My assumption:

If I interrupt Talisa, **then** Talisa won't like me.

However, reality showed me that Talisa *likes* it when I interrupt her.

Later, I found this to be true for more people who speak a lot. Also, numerous people who speak a lot do so out of insecurity. Talking a lot gives them a way to control the situation. I'm not suggesting that you start interrupting everyone. I'm telling you about this situation to demonstrate how harmful assumptions can be. By making assumptions, I was getting frustrated and triggering negative thoughts for the other person too.

Assumptions mess up many relationships, whether business or romantic.

Principle #14:

Minimize your assumptions about the other person. Instead, strive to check them.

My emotional elephant likes to make assumptions and enjoys blaming others. Assuming feels good, because admitting that I don't have all the information suggests that I'm not in control.

Also, blaming others feels protective: "See, I'm not the one making mistakes." These shortcuts feel good in the moment because they temporarily take away discomfort. However, as we have seen, assuming and blaming lead to issues later.

Instead, I could choose a more emotionally intelligent response. First, what information does my rational rider have? The rider knows that I have 45 minutes until my deadline. Last time I worked on a similar task, it took me 40 minutes. Every minute counts. Second, does my emotional elephant have something useful to say? When Talisa started talking to me, I could feel a tension in my stomach. This was my emotional elephant telling me that the deadline is important to me. The emotional elephant whispers in my ear, "You don't want to be in this conversation." Combining facts with feelings tells me that I need to tell Talisa this is not a good time to talk.

When I blamed Talisa, I wasn't only blaming her behavior. I also attributed the negativity to her entire personality. Honestly, the name "Talkative Talisa" came to mind. But of course, Talisa is not a bad person for talking so much. She might just be enthusiastic to see me, because she enjoys socializing with her colleagues. Apparently, she assumed that starting with small talk would be best, while I would have preferred Talisa coming straight to the point.

Most people who display negative behavior don't have bad intentions. My colleague Eric who yelled at his teammate yesterday is not a bad person. His emotion rises because one of his needs is not being met. Perhaps Eric felt he wasn't taken seriously while he wanted to fulfil his need of esteem. He believed that yelling would help him reach that goal. Eric's beliefs and needs form the algorithm that triggers the yelling behavior. Eric does not have bad intentions. He is only displaying one of his Joker algorithms — and don't we all have those?

In such a situation, you can decide to help the other person meet that need or at least show empathy for their emotions. That doesn't mean we should be a doormat, letting people walk over us. You can always set boundaries. The point is, when you understand that most people have good intentions, it's easier to empathize with them. As a result, negative emotions will be reduced, and you can build a strong relationship.

Principle #15:

Most people have good intentions. Behind an unfavorable behavior is usually an unmet need. The belief that the behavior they display will get that need fulfilled is their algorithm.

The interaction between me and Talisa illustrates what can happen if you choose your behavior on premature assumptions. What is the alternative? Become more expressive and let the other person know what's going on in your head.

What does that look like?

Me: "This is not a good time for me to talk. Can we speak later?"

Or Talisa, after seeing me looking out the window: "Am I disturbing you?"

This leads to less misunderstanding, fewer assumptions, and less blame — the basis for open communication.

The principles of this story are applicable in all of your social situations. I'll give you more examples in the next chapter to illustrate how you can learn about other people's algorithms.

CHAPTER 13:
HOW YOU CAN LEARN
ABOUT OTHER PEOPLE'S
ALGORITHMS

Imagine you're browsing on Amazon's website and click on *The Hundred-Page Machine Learning Book* by Andriy Burkov. Amazon tracks your website visit, because that information helps to predict what products you will buy in the future.

The behavior that Amazon can observe on the surface — your page view of the book — gives a bit of information. You may be interested in machine learning. You may be a fan of the author. You may enjoy reading non-fiction books. However, Amazon cannot be sure. With just data about your single page view, it's difficult to make a solid prediction. The prediction will be largely based on assumptions of your behavior. Once Amazon gets more data about you, their estimation of what you need as a customer moves closer to reality.

Why are you looking at this book? Are you only looking around? Or have you decided to buy this book already? Are you interested in buying it for yourself or as a present? Knowing more about the "why" behind your behavior enables Amazon to create a better customer experience.

Human interactions work in the same way. The more often we observe the same person displaying a certain type of behavior, the more certainty we have that this is their default behavioral pattern. If we have observed many times that Talisa starts talking more when the other person looks out of the window, it's likely that she will behave the same way in future. However, if you're only looking at the behavior — the output of the algorithm — you have limited information. In that case, you have no idea why her algorithm chooses "talk more" as the optimal response for the input "my conversation partner is looking away." In other words, we only look at the behavior on the surface; that's why we don't know Talisa's needs and beliefs. As a result, we have no idea how her algorithm processes the input — my behavior.

When you understand the "why" behind the behavior of those around you, you're not only able to better understand their behavior, but you will also be better able to predict how they will behave in other situations.

In summary, the better you understand other people's algorithms, i.e. the *why* underlying their behavior, the better you can predict their behavior, and thus the smoother your interactions become.

Principle #16:

Having a good understanding of other people's algorithms (their beliefs and needs) helps to predict their behavior. This gives you the opportunity to make interactions easier, more productive, and more fun.

So, how can we learn more about the why of other people's behavior? How can we get more information about other people's algorithms? Let's see how Amazon does this. They learn about your beliefs and needs in two ways:

1) Amazon observes your behavior by tracking your clicks (surface-level behavior).

2) Amazon asks for your preferences (below-surface needs).

For example:

1) A page view of a certain book (surface-level behavior).

2) A customer interview in which the customer tells them about his or her preferences (below-surface needs and beliefs).

You can probably guess which one is more valuable. In the first scenario, Amazon only gets a little information that they can use to make assumptions. However, they don't have any certainty that these assumptions are true. The second scenario, a customer interview, will likely give Amazon a deeper understanding of the algorithms of that customer.

Amazon tries to get more data about the people that interact with them. If you want to get better with people, you should aim for the same. The better you understand the other person, the easier the interaction will be.

Like Amazon, you can get more data about other people in two ways:

1) Observe their behavior (surface-level behavior).

2) Ask for their preferences (below-surface beliefs and needs).

1. Observe behavior

One way to learn about the algorithms of other people is by observing their behavior. Remember, this only gives you some information — not the complete picture of the iceberg. Unless you see a certain type of behavior repeating over time, it's challenging to predict the behavior of that person in the future.

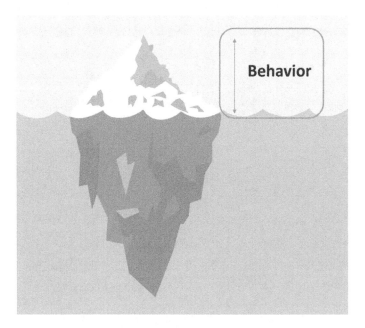

You see human behavior around you all day: in the daily stand-up with your team when your boss gets defensive after being confronted about his overdue task; during a lunch conversation where your colleague speaks passionately about his side project;

on your commute back home where you see that woman smile at others and initiate a conversation.

By becoming a more conscious observer of human behavior, you can learn a lot about other people. The more you learn about them, the better you will be at predicting how people will behave. Better predictions mean smoother interactions.

When observing people, you improve your eye for recognizing nonverbal behavior of people too. To practice, you can watch your favorite series without sound and subtitles. Are you able to understand what's going on?

As mentioned, observations about behavior give us some information on the surface. If we make predictions, these are still based on assumptions, which we want to minimize. To get deeper insights into the driving force behind someone's behavior, we need to ask them about their algorithms. This will give us more information about the beliefs and needs of the other person.

2. Ask someone about their algorithms

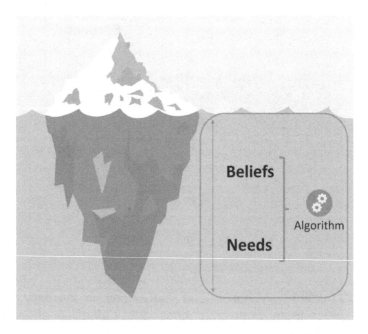

You can ask for other people's algorithms in two ways:

- Literally
- Casually

Asking for their algorithms — literally

One way to get more data about the algorithms of other people is to literally ask them. But what does that mean — literally? Sitting down over a cappuccino and firing the question, "So tell me about your algorithms," is unlikely to get a helpful response. You need to ask the other person high-quality questions.

The questions don't necessarily need to go deep. You don't need to dive straight into the other person's biggest fears and childhood traumas.

When you meet someone who you will work with for at least a few weeks, you can ask one of the following questions:

1) "What is important for you here at work?"

2) "What is important to you in our collaboration?"

These broad questions can reveal a lot about the other person because you allow them to respond in a lot of different ways.

For example, for this question "What is important at work?", the other person could respond as follows:

a) "I find it important to get to know people on a personal level. I like to have lunch with my colleagues and not only talk about work."

b) "I only care about the results. I'm not at work to make friends."

Or the other person may share an opinion:

a) "We need to share what we have learned with the team. So much knowledge goes to waste here. I find that a shame."

b) "We spend so much time sharing knowledge that we forget the actual work. Last month we missed three deadlines. I'm disappointed. This cannot happen again."

The answer tells you which lens they see the world through. From there, you can decide to dig deeper into the topics the other person mentioned. For example, consider the following situation with your manager:

You: "What do you find important in our collaboration?"

Your manager: "Communication is crucial."

You silently wondering: "Communication — what does that even mean?"

You: "What do you mean exactly?"

Your manager: "I want you to give me regular and valuable updates."

After that, you can follow up with more questions:

- **What** information do you need?
- **How** do you want to hear from me? Email, phone call, in-person talk?
- **When** and **how often**?
- **Who**? Is there anyone else I should inform?

When you have the right information, you can thank him for sharing the details and say it will help you communicate effectively with him.

Why is this so effective?

1) You show that you care about your manager's needs. By asking about his preferences, you collect a lot of data that you can use to tailor your communication. Everyone is different. Some people appreciate constant updates; others only want to know if you need help.

2) You show that you are proactive, which is a positive trait for collaborating with others.

3) By discussing this beforehand, you prevent future annoyances.

What would happen if you didn't ask?

Imagine the following situation. Your manager gets tons of emails, and you don't want to further flood his inbox. You assume that the best way is to give an update if you bump into him on the floor.

The result:

Your manager gets annoyed because he never hears from you unless he's running to his next meeting. This is a moment he isn't paying much attention to your needs. Your manager doesn't make the time to discuss your update, because that requires time and he's busy. Hence, your false assumption leads to nonoptimal behavior and counterproductive results.

Asking for their algorithms — casually

Amazon doesn't have time to do interviews with each customer. In a similar way, you may think, "Hey, I have better stuff to do than talk about other people's algorithms." Or maybe you think this could come off as intrusive.

However, you *don't* need to have a formal algorithm conversation to increase your understanding of other people. Even in casual conversations, you can learn a lot about other people's algorithms.

You want to learn about the *why* of their algorithms to understand what's important in their decision-making.

If someone says "I like…"

For example:

"I like to work here."

"I liked that project."

"I liked my holiday in Spain."

Then always ask:

"*What* do you like about it?"

The answer will give you much information about the other person.

For example:

"I like to work here because many people are direct. I don't like beating around the bush."

These two sentences give you a lot of information about how the person wants to be treated. Next time when you give that person constructive criticism, don't spend minutes on introducing your feedback. Instead, get to the point.

Through this simple question, "What do you like about it?", you achieve three things:

1) You get valuable data about the other person, which you can use to tailor your communication.

2) The question puts the other person in a good mood because people enjoy talking about things they like.

3) The question gives the other person the opportunity to talk about him or herself. And that's what many people enjoy. Diana Tamir and Jason Mitchell, both PhDs at Harvard University, monitored the brain activity of participants who talked about themselves.[21] Their observations were striking. The participants had increased activity in the brain regions associated with pleasure. These are the areas that also get triggered when we get pleasure from food, money, or sex.

As mentioned, by asking good questions, you get a lot of information about other people's algorithms. Next to that, most likely you will pick up on hobbies and interests outside of work too. You can use these as topics for future conversations and therefore build a stronger relationship.

Exercise #7:

■ *Ask people for their algorithms.*

In your next conversation today, ask people for their algorithms. Try to be curious about what people enjoy and what they find important. This understanding allows you to make small adjustments in your communication style and thereby improve collaboration and build strong relationships.

Make predictions

By observing and asking about people's algorithms, you get a lot of information about them. Want to have some fun?

Use this set of information to make predictions about other people's behavior.

Keep in mind that these are predictions and thus based on assumptions.

Here are a few examples of predictions you could make:

- A lady from another department makes a remark about the performance of your team. Your colleague leans forward. What do you think he's thinking? What is he going to say next?

- Your boss pitches a new idea. How do you think colleague X will respond? Based on what your colleague mentioned in previous meetings, will he be in favor of the idea? If not, will he speak up?

- That client gives direct feedback to your colleague. How do you think she will react? Will your colleague receive the feedback well, like last month when you gave her feedback? Or will she get defensive, as she mentioned to you that she prefers a more indirect style?

Now it's up to you! It's like a little game, predicting how people will respond. Over time, you'll get better at it. Even the most unpredictable people will have patterns that you can recognize.

When your prediction is wrong, that's okay. This mistake gives you more observational data, which will help you make a better prediction next time.

Note: this game is only intended for you as an observer. Before acting on your predictions, always strive to check your assumptions with the people involved.

Principle #17:

You can learn about people's algorithms in different ways. Observing behavior will only give you surface-level information. Asking about other people's algorithms often leads to a deeper understanding, which in turn will improve your social interactions.

CHAPTER 14:
DEALING WITH
"DIFFICULT" BEHAVIOR

Understanding other people's algorithms helps us predict their behavior. However, that does not mean we always enjoy the behavior of others. Do you agree? Especially the behavior of people who are different from us (i.e. people who have other types of algorithms). But how fair is our judgment of the behavior of others?

As Stephen Covey said, "We judge ourselves by our intentions. And others by their actions."[22]

This chapter helps you to deal with the "difficult" behavior of other people.

Generally, we find it easier to understand the behavior of people who have a personality comparable to ours. Also, we tend to like people who are similar to us.[23]

Whether you like it or not, people you meet will judge you. They will make judgments about your trustworthiness within a tenth of second.[24] They even use body odor to determine whether you should be placed in the category "friend" or "foe."[25] And of course, you do too.

These quick verdicts were useful in medieval times, where the prediction of trustworthiness helped us to survive. However, in today's world, this labeling based on fluffy assumptions can harm the relationships we develop at work.

Why? Because of the confirmation bias, a tendency to search for or interpret information in a way that confirms our prior personal beliefs.[26] Unfortunately, this bias makes us falsely confirm our hypotheses in social situations too.[27] In other words, after our initial judgment, we look for evidence that our judgment was right.

For example, we decide in the first second that a colleague we meet is not competent. An hour later, we see that he waits for a few seconds before answering a question. Then we see our initial belief confirmed: "See, I was right. He doesn't know the answer — he is incompetent." Because we see all the actions of the colleague through the lens of incompetence, it's hard to keep an open mind about his behavior in the future. In contrast, with an open mind, we could have interpreted the silence as a sign of strength.

Who is responsible for these quick judgments? Of course, this is our emotional brain, trying to take shortcuts. Become aware of these tendencies and try to stay objective.

As Robert Greene writes in his book *The Laws of Human Nature*, "If you are observing someone you naturally dislike, or who reminds you of someone unpleasant in your past, you will tend to see almost any cue as unfriendly or hostile. You will do the opposite for people you like. In these exercises you must strive to subtract your personal preferences and prejudices about people."[28]

As we are tempted to like people who are similar to us, it can help to focus on commonalities instead of differences. Remember Maslow's hierarchy? Deep down, we all have the same type of needs. People who observe differences in others are less likely to enjoy interacting with them. Hence, if you're observing someone who you dislike, you will tend to see almost any cue as unfriendly.

Also, if you don't like someone, maybe you just don't know that person well enough. This thinking is in line with Abraham Lincoln's philosophy. He once expressed these compelling words, "I don't like that man. I must get to know him better."

Principle #18:

Stay away from quick judgments about other people, because they harm the ability to build relationships at work.

We are more likely to misunderstand people who are different from us. That's why we are tempted to label them as "difficult." In doing so, we place them in a different category and are even less likely to appreciate their behavior. Before you know it, you are pulled into the cycle of assumptions and blame, which I explained in the example with Talisa.

As an alternative, we could see the other person as human, with their own set of fears and flaws. That makes it easier to empathize with them. What works for me is to think about the other person as an innocent child. Everyone was an innocent child at some point, and we formed algorithms that will protect us against the difficult side of life. Our "negative" behavior often arises when we are most scared or hurt.

Imagine that you work on a project and — due to reasons out of your control — you need to push the final deadline one week back. Your colleague, Victor, depends on the outcome of your project. When you tell him about the new deadline, he explodes in anger. His emotions erupt like lava from a volcano. Now, the easy path would be to judge him, to gossip and tell your colleagues about "Volcano Victor." However, is there a different way you can respond? Possibly, he was a big fan of going to the playground in his childhood, but his parents kept postponing the day they would go. Or maybe Victor has an enormous commitment for this project, and the new deadline makes him anxious about failing.

Seeing the other person as an innocent child can make you more compassionate. This makes it easier to see that there are no bad intentions behind the hostile behaviors of others. Instead, you can see the fear of an anxious toddler, desperately screaming for belonging and esteem. By having a more empathetic viewpoint, you keep the connection, even if the other person's personality is your polar opposite. This connection helps you build a trusting relationship. In contrast, throwing bricks of judgment builds a wall between you and the other person.

Entirely eliminating judgments may be too great a hurdle. Kegan and Lahey, authors of the book *Immunity to Change,* offer a smaller step. They suggest to focus on the positive aspects of the person we are judging to balance the negatives.[29] For example:

- "She may be screaming at me right now, but she knows a lot about this topic."
- "He is pushy, but he's often the first to offer help."

If you can't think of anything positive about the other person's personality, start with a trivial attribute. For example:

- "She doesn't show any interest in others, but her handwriting is magnificent."

- "He is extremely arrogant, but his shoes always look fashionably on point."

Having such an empathetic viewpoint doesn't mean that you need to accept behavior that crosses your boundaries. You can always have a conversation with the other person to draw a line. The point is, such a conversation is more productive when you understand that, in most cases, the other person has not got bad intentions. The behavior is simply an attempt to get their needs met, because that's how they learned to get their needs met in the past. Your arrogant colleague may be showing off to try to get their need for esteem and recognition met. Perhaps people complimented him in the past, and that made him feel good.

I have presented two strategies for dealing with people who are different from you:

1) Seeing the other person as an innocent child.

2) Focusing on positive points of their personality.

These strategies can help make your interactions with difficult people at least manageable. To take it one step further, we can learn a lot from people who are different from us. How? I'll explain with an example.

We can learn a lot from people who are different from us

In my first job after university, I had a colleague, let's call her Barbara, who was vastly different from me. One day, I saw a colleague approach Barbara and ask if she could help with a certain task. Barbara's answer? "No."

That is it. No explanation. No justification. Just, "No." This was an eye-opener for me. I could hardly imagine this was possible, because I struggled to say no. Watching someone say that word so effortlessly was a great learning experience.

Some situations may ask for a more diplomatic response — a style that's more natural to me. At the end of the project, I had a conversation with Barbara, in which she told me that she learned a lot from my style during situations of conflicts. Apparently, the learning went both ways.

We have a natural tendency to spend time with people that are similar to us, because we like them and it's easier to understand them. However, if you only spend time with people who are similar, you're missing out on learning opportunities.

To conclude, next time you are working together with someone you don't like, sense the impulses of your emotional elephant. Instead of judging their behavior, try to see the other person as an innocent child, trying to protect themselves from hurting. See if you can appreciate how the other person is different from you, no matter how hard it might be. Spend your energy on finding chances to learn instead of opportunities to blame.

Principle #19:

You can learn a lot, perhaps the most, from people who are different from you.

CHAPTER 15:
NICE GUY BEHAVIOR

So far, Part 3 helped you get a deep understanding of other people's algorithms, that is, a strong awareness of their preferences. You could use this information to carefully choose your behavior exactly in line with their preferences.

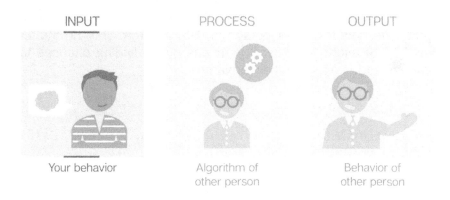

INPUT	PROCESS	OUTPUT
Your behavior	Algorithm of other person	Behavior of other person

No stepping on toes. No upsetting people. No confrontations. Isn't that great? Well, as you can probably sense, there's a dark side to this story.

Once you better understand how someone else prefers to communicate, you can make small adjustments to your communication style. This can help you collaborate better with your colleagues — just like we saw in the example with our manager in chapter 13. Not only can verbal modifications ease your communication with others, but mirroring body language can also help you build relationships with other people.[30]

Making these subtle modifications in your way of communication doesn't mean you throw your character overboard. The goal of learning about other people's algorithms is not 100% about adjusting our behavior. If you're changing your whole character based on the people around you, people have no idea who you are. If you try to please everybody, nobody will be pleased.

Nice Guy

Do you know the concept of the "nice guy"? You may have heard about it, but probably not in the way I will explain it. There are many nice guys (and girls!) in the world, who seem very nice. On the surface, at least.

Below are a few examples of nice guy behavior:

Behavior	Examples
Put the needs of other people first	"We can go with your idea."
Give away decision-making power	"No, you choose the restaurant. I'm okay with anything."
Modify feedback	"Yes, the food was good, thank you." (To the waiter after a terrible meal)
Withhold opinions	"Hmm… My view clashes with hers. I won't say I disagree, so I can keep the conversation positive."
Conceal emotions	"It's okay." (When your colleague arrives late for the third time in a row. Deep inside, you are angry.)
Hide "strange" hobbies	"I won't mention my passion for writing and personal development. He may think it's weird."

How do I know this?

Because these are personal examples. I was an enormous nice guy in the past. I was continually withholding my thoughts or changing my words to please other people. However, my understanding of other people's algorithms was wrong. I had a false belief because I thought "If I'm nice to people, then they will like me and we will have a good relationship."

This is a wrong assumption, because most people prefer to interact with those who honestly say what they think, even if the thoughts clash with their own view. Pleasing the other person may lead to harmony in the short term. However, continually calculating your optimal behavior based on what you know about other people's algorithms leads to serious issues in the long run.

As a nice guy, I was continually making modifications to my behavior — often subtle changes; sometimes huge adjustments. I wasn't aware of it, but I gave up my own opinions and compromised my personal values many times. As a result, people didn't know who I really was and what I stood for. Some people didn't respect me, because I was afraid to speak the truth. Others didn't trust me, because I acted so calculated and robotic. This lack of trust was an enormous obstacle in building strong relationships with the people around me.

This nice guy behavior not only took a toll on my relationships, but it also harmed the results I wanted to achieve in the office. While I'm a pretty ambitious guy, others were not always as driven as I was. We agreed on deadlines, and they kept missing them. And what did I say? "Okay. When do you think you can finish it?" Sometimes this cycle repeated two or three times without me expressing that I wasn't happy with it. I was frustrated that we didn't make progress as fast. However, I kept all this emotion inside.

Getting rid of this type of pleasing behavior was a battle for me. The popularity of the book *No More Mr. Nice Guy* by Robert Glover indicates that I wasn't the only one struggling.[31] This book is not about business, but if you want to get rid of your pleasing behavior, it can help you tremendously in your professional life.

At first sight, nice guys seem nice because they put a lot of effort into keeping the interaction positive. However, their motives under the surface are everything but nice. Nice guy behavior is not only based on the false misconception that other people enjoy pleasing behavior, but also, although many nice guys aren't aware, technically their behavior may be driven by dishonest and selfish motives.

Nice guys don't have the confidence that they will be okay if their views clash with others'. Being overly sensitive for the need to belong, nice guys neglect what they find important, to make sure they don't upset anyone. They pretend things are okay while they're holding a grudge inside. This anger will transform into resentment toward people around them. Is that fair?

In other words, nice guys act like chameleons. They change colors to match their surroundings. Nice guys hide their true color; they do everything to avoid conflict and rejection. They behave as if they are still living in an ancient tribe, in which confrontations could be deadly. Nice guys eagerly want to be liked and believe that pleasing other people will get other people to like them. Well, how nice is that?

David Brooks, author of *The Social Animal*, also wrote about people who are unwilling to tell the painful truth. He calls it "the dishonesty of niceness." He says, "The desire not to cause pain was just an unwillingness to have an unpleasant conversation. It was cowardice, not consideration."[32]

Principle #20:

When you deeply understand the algorithms of other people, you know exactly how to please other people with your behavior. However, this nice guy act is based on the wrong understanding of other people's algorithms. Most people don't enjoy such pleasing behavior, and that's why it leads to serious issues in the long term.

Be honest to yourself. Do you recognize yourself — even a tiny bit — in the nice guy behaviors described here?

You may think, "Hey, this isn't me. I'm always acting independently, without being influenced by the people around me." In this case, I have an interesting piece of research for you. You may adjust your behavior more than you think.

In the experiment of Solomon Asch, participants were asked to judge which comparison line (A, B, or C) was most like the target line. The answer was always obvious. As you can see, in the following example, the correct answer is C.

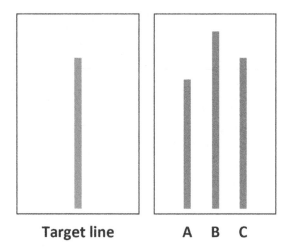

Target line   **A B C**

The participants invited thought they were in a group with other participants. In reality, however, there was only one real participant in each group. The other seven participants were actors. They had agreed to all choose the same (wrong) option for 12 critical rounds out of the 18 in total. The real participant didn't know this and was the last person to give the answer.

Overall, 75% of the participants gave at least one wrong answer out of the 12 critical rounds. In the control group, without any actors, less than 1% of the participants gave a wrong answer. What a difference! In interviews after the experiment, most of the participants said they didn't really believe their conforming answers but were afraid of being ridiculed.[33]

These results are a good reminder to reflect on your own behavior: how much are you influenced by the people around you? If you recognize some of the pleasing nice guy behavior, you certainly adjust a lot to your surroundings. In that case, a next logical question is about the alternative: what is the opposite of the nice guy?

The opposite of a nice guy

Is it a bad boy?

No.

I would describe bad boys (or girls) as people who don't care about others. They are arrogant, manipulative, and push people around, completely caught up in their own world. That doesn't sound like a good alternative.

Instead, I call the opposite of a nice guy a "MindSpeaker". A MindSpeaker can be a man or woman. Gender doesn't matter. Attitude does. A MindSpeaker doesn't have the same false belief as the nice guy. A MindSpeaker understands the algorithms of others and knows that pleasing everybody is not a good strategy in the long run.

That's why a MindSpeaker says what's on his mind. He listens well and is open to other people's perspectives. At the same time, a MindSpeaker says what he is thinking, even if his views clash with those of others. A MindSpeaker expresses his feelings, because feelings aren't weak, but reveal that we are human.

A MindSpeaker speaks the truth and is authentic. He doesn't avoid conflict, because he knows that he will be okay. A MindSpeaker doesn't nervously avoid stepping on other people's toes. A MindSpeaker understands that social tension and disagreement are healthy and can lead to deep relationships and new business insights. A MindSpeaker takes the initiative and isn't afraid to make mistakes, because he knows he isn't perfect. A MindSpeaker cares more about learning than about the judgments of others.

A MindSpeaker understands that it's healthy to have needs. That's why he draws boundaries assertively. He strives to be clear to others, instead of being vague about what he wants. A MindSpeaker tells others about his own algorithms and gives feedback to others, because he wants to give others the opportunity to understand his preferences.

A MindSpeaker cares. He is nice to others, not because he tries to manipulate others into liking him, but because he thinks that's the right thing to do. A MindSpeaker prioritizes inner values over outer reputation.

If you recognize yourself in some of the nice guy behaviors, you may wonder how you can get rid of those patterns. Transforming from a nice guy to a MindSpeaker isn't easy, but if you continually follow the steps from Part 2 (Optimize), you will get there.

1) **Catch yourself:** Take a pause when your nice guy behavior is triggered. Do you feel an urge to please, to take away tension or to avoid conflict?

2) **Experiment with different behavior:** Express your needs, reveal your emotions, say no, try to be free of the positive and negative opinions of others.

3) **Repeat and monitor results:** You don't transform overnight. Step by step, the new behavior will be more automatic to you, and you will transform into a MindSpeaker. Consistency is key in building your new algorithms.

I can imagine if this seems challenging. In Part 4, we will elaborate on how you can tell other people about your algorithms.

In conclusion, when you have a deep understanding of the algorithms of others, you can predict how others will respond to your behavior. However, that doesn't mean that always carefully choosing the desirable behavior to please others is a good strategy. This strategy is based on a wrong assumption, because most people don't enjoy such pleasing behavior.

Earlier in this book, I mentioned that it's wise to evaluate your algorithms every now and then. That doesn't mean you should analyze each social situation while you're in it. Strategically choosing your optimal behavior for each move will make you come across as robotic. That makes it hard for others to relate to you. Instead, get out of your head. Do not think so much, and do trust your feelings. This is how you can get the best of both worlds — being spontaneous in your daily interactions, and regularly taking a step back to optimize your algorithms.

CONCLUSION PART 3

In this part, we discussed the driving forces behind other people's algorithms. By observing the behavior of others and asking about their preferences, you can improve your collaboration with them. It's important that you minimize assumptions, because these are the source of misunderstanding and social friction. Better to look at the tip of the iceberg and ask what is below the surface. That's where you can find the underlying beliefs and needs of the other person. When you have a deep understanding of the algorithms of others, you can strategically choose your behavior so that others will be pleased. However, such nice guy behavior leads to serious issues in the long run. As the last part of this book will demonstrate, there are other methods that are much more effective in increasing your influence.

PART 4

INFLUENCE: STEER OTHER PEOPLE'S BEHAVIOR

INTRODUCTION

Understanding your own algorithms and becoming more self-aware was the start of everything. Changing your behavior, reprograming your mind to build better algorithms, was the second part. Understanding other people's algorithms, looking under the iceberg and discovering people's needs and beliefs, was the third part.

The first three parts were vital to learn about our own behavior and how we can best interact with others. Now we can take the next step and build our road to influence. It's going to be an exciting journey. This part focuses on steering other people's behavior.

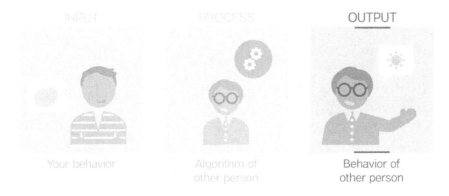

INPUT   PROCESS   OUTPUT

Your behavior   Algorithm of   Behavior of
                 other person   other person

As mentioned, in this book, the approach for influence doesn't build on a basis of manipulation. Instead, we'll focus on transparency and mutual gains. To clarify what I mean with manipulation, let's look at a hypothetical scenario with my colleague, who I will call Sandra.

From the outside she looks like a modern businesswoman. Neat shoes. Beautiful dress pants. Perfectly matching jacket. But from the inside, Sandra is the finest example of a prehistoric cave woman. She has an extreme fear that the tribe will reject her. As a result, Sandra is extremely sensitive to positive feedback. Thank you, evolution.

Now, let's see what happens when she gives a presentation. To me, Sandra comes across as nervous, and the presentation lacks a clear message. But the thing is, I want to ask for Sandra's help later, because she has certain knowledge that I need. Also, I have a great understanding of her algorithms — she loves to get compliments.

Imagine I walk up to Sandra after the meeting and say, "That was a great presentation! Well done." Like I predicted, she is extremely pleased.

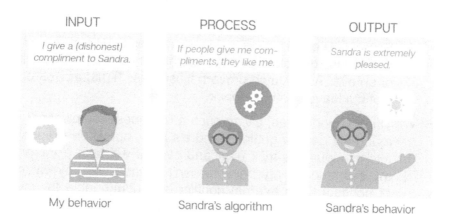

Then, later that afternoon, I ask for her help. In her decision whether to help me or not, she will take into account the positive feeling she got when I gave her the compliment. Sandra anticipates that I will give her more positive feedback in the future. Therefore, she agrees to help me.

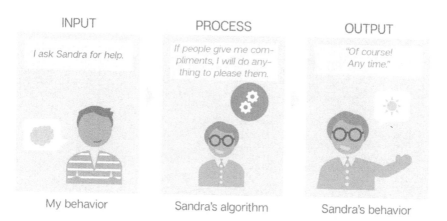

The results:

1) Sandra is happy. She feels good about herself.

2) I am happy. I will receive Sandra's help.

We are both happy and reached our goals. Isn't that great? No.

- First, this doesn't help Sandra develop her presentation skills.

- Second, even if I have a long business relationship with Sandra, my dishonesty can break the connection in the blink of an eye. As a Dutch proverb illustrates, "Trust arrives on foot but leaves on horseback."

- Third, how do I feel giving such a dishonest compliment? I reach my goal of getting Sandra's help, but when I repeat this manipulative trick over and over, it will take a toll on my self-respect. My behavior isn't aligned with my value of honesty. This internal conflict is uncomfortable for my emotional elephant. That's why he will send a signal. I can feel in my stomach that such behavior isn't right.

Looking at this example, manipulation isn't the best way to steer the behavior of other people. Then, what is a better alternative?

In this part of the book, I'll explain how you can influence people in a more honest way.

CHAPTER 16:
WHY YOU SHOULD SHARE YOUR DATA

To kick off this chapter, let's look at a quote by Or Skolnik, partner at Bain Consulting,

"When I buy a new car, it comes with a user manual, so I know how to operate it. But when I work with a new person, who is way more complex than a car, I don't get anything."

That means every time you meet someone who you will interact with at work, you have to start from zero. Even though the other person has all these experiences that could help you understand how the person works, you need to find out from scratch how you can best interact with them. That's why Skolnik decided to write his personal user manual: a one-pager on how to work with him effectively. What are his strengths? What are his weaknesses? What are the triggers that bring out the best and worst in him?

In this way, Skolnik shares pieces of data about his personality with his colleagues. That's how they learn more about his algorithms. His idea is in line with the philosophy of a MindSpeaker: not being afraid to express thoughts and feelings. By speaking your mind, you not only come across as more authentic, but you also teach others what's important to you. As a result, people may take your preferences into account — and so you influence their behavior. Note that this in their own interests too, because you help people understand how they can best interact with you. Wouldn't it be helpful if you knew how best to interact with each individual colleague?

Principle #21:

Working together with someone you don't know well can be difficult. Collaborating is easier when you let others know how best to work with you.

People would like to know your preferences

To underline Skolnik's point, let's imagine the following scenario. Your colleague is designing a new mobile application that you and your team expect to use every day.

The designer is Daniel, and he sits in the same office. When you stand up from your seat, you see him working on the large table. It's the creative guy with the red shoes.

In front of Daniel is a large piece of paper with the interaction design of the mobile application. Above Daniel's table, you see a large sign saying "Please walk by and tell me how you prefer to interact."

You know you will use the application every day. Now you face a decision: do you walk over to Daniel to give him your requirements? Or do you stay quiet, just hoping that he will guess them correctly?

If you do walk over to Daniel, he'll be able to take your preferences into account. That would make your interactions with the application much easier:

1) The topics of your interest appear more frequently at the top, personalized to your taste.

2) The interface is in line with your preference. You know where all the buttons are.

3) The application only talks to you when you want it. No annoying notifications when you're working on your deadline with full concentration.

People don't have a "Please tell me how you prefer to interact" sign above their heads. However, everyone wants better social interactions. And the more other people know about your algorithms, the more opportunities they have for improving interactions with you. Don't keep your preferences to yourself because you're afraid to bother the other person. Instead, realize that sharing your preferences helps the other person understand you!

Of course, you never know whether other people will take your preferences into account. However, if you don't share your preferences, you don't even give them the opportunity.

This famous quote floats around on the internet, "The definition of insanity is doing the same thing over and over again and expecting a different result."

Many people debate whether it was Einstein who said it. I don't really care who said it. I like the quote, but I have a different definition: the definition of insanity is not sharing your preferences while expecting others to take them into account.

According to that definition, I was pretty insane in the past.

Remember the conversation with Talisa? I thought, "How can you not see that this is not the right time to talk?" Insanity, insanity.

I'm the only one responsible for helping other people learn about my preferences.

If I'm blaming other people, I give away all my power.

Instead, if I ask myself, "What can *I* do to improve the situation?", all of the power is within me. I can change the situation by expressing my needs.

Eventually, I was able to break the insanity wall between Talisa and me. I told her that I needed time to focus and that I had no time to talk. Because I was transparent about my algorithms, I gave Talisa the opportunity to take my preferences into account.

Now, I'm curious. In your next interactions with your colleague, will you share your preferences? Remember, your colleague would love to hear from you.

Other benefits of sharing more of your data

For many years, I kept data about my personality close to me. I was cautious sharing my data. I didn't want to come across as an attention-seeker, talking about myself a lot. Instead, I wanted communication to be brief and efficient. I only shared my preferences when people asked for them, instead of sharing them proactively. In that way, I was acting like a poker player, not showing my cards if it wasn't required. As a result, people couldn't take my collaboration preferences into account. And that wasn't the only benefit I missed out on. There are two more advantages of sharing your data:

1) **Sharing more about yourself helps you to build relationships.**

Susan Sprecher, professor of sociology, studied the effect of sharing personal details, like hobbies and favorite childhood memories. In her research, she found that sharing personal details can make you come across as warmer and more likable. Only listening and showing interest by asking questions isn't enough.

Research from Sprecher stated, "Although shy or socially anxious people may ask questions of the other to detract attention from themselves, our research shows that this is not a good strategy for relationship initiation. Both participants in an interaction need to disclose to generate mutual closeness and liking."[34]

Hence, both people in the conversation need to take turns with self-disclosure for it to have a positive effect.

2) **Telling others about your preferences makes you more self-aware.**

Every time you express your preferences, you are forced to think about them. A vague thought in your mind is different from a spoken sentence. Verbalizing your preferences makes you more aware. What exactly is my preference? Has my preference changed since I thought about it last time?

In summary, there are various benefits of sharing more of your data. The next chapter demonstrates how sharing your data works in practice.

CHAPTER 17:
HOW TO SHARE YOUR ALGORITHMS

As we discussed in Part 3, your needs and beliefs are the driving force behind your algorithms. They are the pieces of data that help others understand how your algorithms work. Thus, when you share your beliefs and needs with other people, they learn more about your algorithms. People can then take your needs into account when they interact with you.

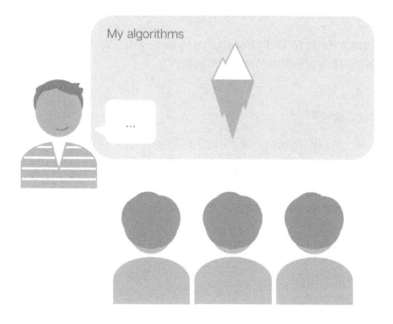

You can tell others about your algorithms in two ways:

1) **Proactively:** before the other person's behavior occurs

2) **Reactively:** after the other person's behavior occurs

1) Share your data proactively: tell people about your algorithms

The first option is to share your data proactively. In other words, you tell people what type of behavior you appreciate and what type of behavior you find challenging to deal with.

One way to do this is to share your data in a highly organized way. An example is the personal user manual that Skolnik created. I don't have a complete personal user manual, but I did create a list of points that make collaborating with me effective. I call this list my "Keys to Collaboration":

1) Give me the freedom and time to come up with new ideas. Support me when I need help in working them out.

2) Show interest in what I'm thinking. Ask for my opinion and listen.

3) I am curious and constantly want to learn. Be honest in your feedback and share your perspective openly.

Everyone's Keys to Collaboration are different. What are your three key points to work with you effectively?

Exercise #8:

■ *Write down your Keys to Collaboration.*

Take 5 minutes to think how you want others to interact with you. What do you need to make a collaboration successful? Write your Keys to Collaboration down below.

My Keys to Collaboration:

....

....

....

Of course, how you share your Keys to Collaboration matters. Bossing people around without being considerate of their feelings is unlikely to be successful. Don't forget that everyone has a different user manual — everyone has built their own set of algorithms. Presenting your own preferences as a universal truth is likely to trigger the other person's emotional elephant. Instead, ask if they are willing to take your algorithms into account and say that you realize that they may have different preferences. Don't forget to ask about their algorithms too — this is what we discussed in Part 3: Interact. By doing so, you turn a monologue into a dialogue with the topic: *how can we best collaborate?*

Sharing a structured list of your preferences helps people understand how best to interact with you. Ideally, you combine this organized method with a more flexible approach: you weave information about your algorithms into your conversations starting in your first interactions. What does that look like?

Imagine a lunch with colleagues where a new person joins the team. Often, the small talk goes something like this:

Experienced Erica: "Welcome! Where did you work before?"

New Nicholas: "Company X."

Erica: "Interesting. For how long?"

Nicholas: "Three years. What role do you work in?"

Erica: "I am responsible for Y."

Nicholas: "That's nice."

Erica and Nicholas take another bite of their lunch and awkwardly look around to find a new conversation.

(…)

How much information do they have about each other's algorithms?

Whether you're the new person or welcoming the new person, there are many ways to change this conversation.

How? By planting more conversational seeds, which the other person can use to grow the conversation in different directions. For example:

Experienced Erica: "Welcome! Where did you work before?"

New Nicholas: "I worked for Company X. It was a good place to start my career, because I learned a lot from two seniors in my team."

Erica: "Interesting. How long did you work there?"

Nicholas: "Three years. I wanted to switch companies because I didn't have opportunities in the field I want to grow in. My ambition is to work in data science. I like to find patterns and visualize them in a clear way. What is your role here?"

Do you see the difference? By giving more extensive answers, Nicholas planted more conversational seeds.

This is how he gave Erica the opportunity to ask more questions. For example:

1) "What did you learn most from the seniors?"

2) "How come your previous company didn't have any opportunities?"

3) "Why do you like to find patterns and visualize them?"

4) "What led you to change your ambition?"

5) "What do you think is the most important skill for a data scientist?"

Alternatively, based on what you say, Erica could tell Nicholas about her own experience:

1) She could share what she learned from seniors in the beginning of her career.

2) She could tell him about research that shows how valuable mentors are in the first years of your career.

3) She could talk about her own career switch.

4) She could express her admiration for people in data science because she got a bad grade in math in high school.

5) Underline the importance of visualizing information and tell a business story where this failed.

By planting conversational seeds, Nicholas gives Erica more background about his life. Slowly, that gives Erica the opportunity to learn about his algorithms. Moreover, it gives Erica many ways to respond to Nicholas.

Initially, I was closed in my interactions with others — I would overthink every word I wanted to say. "Is this valuable enough for the conversation?" "How will I come across?" In that way, I was cautious about sharing my data. I thought that everything I said needed to be of high quality. Later, I found out there is a lot of value in sharing more context instead of one-word answers. I also realized I'm not an attention-seeker when I tell people more about myself. That's why I started to talk more without overthinking every word. As a result, I started planting more conversational seeds, and I became less mysterious, more interesting. I didn't just give the "correct" answer. Instead, I gave an answer that told others more about me.

If you meet someone new, you are a big puzzle. By sharing pieces of that puzzle, you make life a bit easier for others, and they are able to predict you better. When people don't know about your algorithms, they will make assumptions — and that's what we want to avoid.

Principle #22:

Share more of your personal data in regular conversations. These conversational seeds make it easier for others to understand your algorithms. Moreover, they help the other person develop an interesting dialogue.

Exercise #9:

■ *Share your data in conversations with others. Tell them about your background, interests, and personal preferences.*

In your next conversation today, share a bit more of your background and personal preferences. Remember that your job isn't to precisely answer the question. Instead, your job is to give a response that's useful or fun. By giving more extensive answers, you plant many conversational seeds. These conversational seeds not only help the other person to learn more about your preferences, but they also help the other person develop an interesting dialogue.

Here are a few practical ideas you could share in your conversations:

- *What is important to you at work*

- *What your communication preferences are*

- *What type of projects you were happiest in*

- *What you found most challenging in your previous job*

2) Sharing your data reactively: giving feedback

The previous section covered why it's important to tell others how your algorithms work, even before they start communicating with you. However, that doesn't mean your job is over. To help others understand whether their behavior is desirable, you need to give them continuous feedback. In that way, you create the following loop:

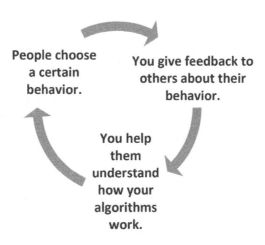

People choose a certain behavior.

You give feedback to others about their behavior.

You help them understand how your algorithms work.

You can respond to that feedback with either positive feedback or constructive criticism. Receiving feedback isn't easy, but giving feedback in an effective way is difficult too. To increase the chances of the other person taking your feedback into account in the future, here are a few guidelines:

Positive feedback:

1) Express appreciation.

2) Specify how it helped you. The more specific, the better.

For example, "Thank you for helping me with the analysis. It was great that you challenged my hypothesis, because it helped me formulate a better one."

Many people say, "Thank you," but never share what helped them exactly.

That's a shame, because a specific compliment has more emotional impact on the other person. Moreover, it helps the other person discover their personal strengths.

Constructive criticism:

1) Give factual observation: describe objective facts, be concrete.

2) Explain their impact on you: say the impact of their behavior.

3) Tell them the behavior you desire: say what behavior you would like to see in the future.

For example, "Yesterday during the team meeting, you interrupted me twice when I presented my idea. As a result, I felt uneasy. Next time, can you let me finish speaking please?"

The goal is to help them understand the impact of their behavior on you. In that way they learn more about your algorithms. You give them the opportunity to adjust their behavior in your interests.

Be mindful with the third step. Giving someone a suggestion for a behavior change often triggers resentment and resistance. Especially when the other person didn't ask you for feedback. Thus, doing only the first two steps may be more effective. In this case, you only tell them about your observation and its impact on you. When the person who receives the feedback comes up with a behavior change themselves, they often feel more valued because the other person hasn't tried to change them, and their behavioral change is more likely to last.

CHAPTER 18: WALKING TO THE OTHER SIDE OF THE TABLE

The previous chapter explained how you can tell people about your algorithms and how you can give feedback to others. In these methods, we mainly considered our own needs. While expressing your personal preferences can help to steer the behavior of others, you need to take one more step to reach your maximum influence potential. In order to skyrocket your influence, you need to look beyond your own goals; you need to link what *you* want to what the *other person* wants.

This sounds simple, but it's not easy. Two cognitive biases make this exercise particularly challenging.

1) The illusion of asymmetric insight

Do you know your colleagues well? Do you know them better than they know you?

Yes? Think again.

Research demonstrates that people are biased to think that they know others better than others know them.[35] In other words, many people falsely believe, "You don't know me, but I do know you."

Principle #23:

You may not know people as well as you think you do.

This bias is known as the "illusion of asymmetric insight."

It has serious consequences. And it's not our only bias either.

2) The false consensus effect

A few years ago, a friend of mine asked me, "What are the biggest mistakes you've made in dealing with people?" I have made many mistakes. But there is one mistake that still makes me laugh: I assumed that other people think in a similar way to me.

Research tells me I'm not the only one making this mistake. According to Lee Ross's research in 1977, people tend to overestimate how much other people think the same way as we do. Even though others have different beliefs and preferences, we are inclined to think that they agree with our way of thinking. This bias is known as the "false consensus effect."[36]

> *Principle #24:*
>
> *Many people think in a way that's vastly different from your way of thinking.*

I have understood this on a theoretical level for many years. But only for a few years have I thoroughly understood what it means when interacting with other people.

Because this is crucial in all your social situations, let me repeat again: most people think in a way that's totally different from your way of thinking. They see and experience the world from a totally different perspective. Other people don't just look through a different pair of glasses; they see things from a totally different angle too. This is important to understand; otherwise you will make the same mistakes I've made. Many, many times I didn't understand other people and I made assumptions about them. This only drove me further away from understanding and getting the results I was looking for.

Let's make this more concrete with an example.

Imagine you are sitting at a table with a colleague in a cafe, about to order lunch. You are having a heated discussion as you can't agree on what you are seeing.

You say: "It's 19."

He says: "No, you're wrong."

You: "No, really, it's 19!"

He thinks: "I can't believe it. It's so clear."

Then he says: "Come here!"

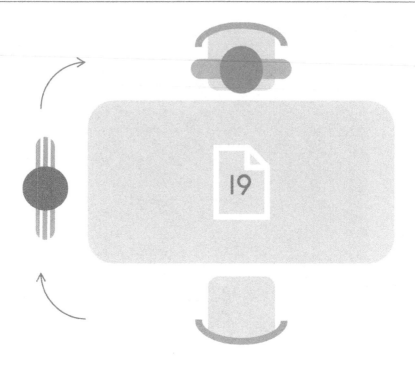

You decide to walk to his side of the table.

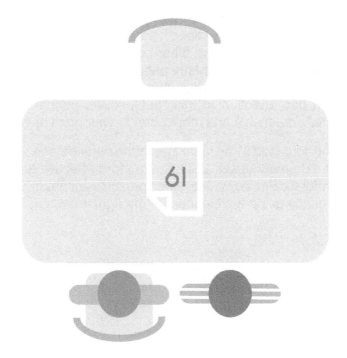

You say: "Hmm, interesting, the world looks different from here. I see what you mean now."

This example may seem simplistic to you. And maybe it is simplistic. But soon, you will understand why this metaphor is so powerful.

In most situations, there are multiple ways of looking at things. When you and your colleague are both arguing from a different point of view, it's difficult to see what your colleague is talking about. The illusion of asymmetric insight makes this even harder, because we think we know others better than they know us. We think we already understand what they want to say. You won't walk a mile in someone's shoes when you think you already know what their shoes feel like.

Then, what is the best strategy? Don't fall for the illusion of asymmetric insight and false consensus effect. Don't assume you already know what the other person thinks. Instead, be willing to walk over to the other side of the table. You may find that the other person's perspective teaches you something new.

Even if there is only one correct answer and you are 100% sure you are right, it can still help to walk to the other side of the table. This is true even if it's only to show that you're willing to see the world from the other person's perspective. However, that doesn't mean that you agree with what the other person is saying. It just shows that you're willing to listen. Many people have a strong urge to feel understood, because it makes them feel valued and important. When you pay attention to their perspective, people will usually become less defensive and more open to your point of view.

Staying on your side of the table makes the other person's emotional elephant extremely upset. Usually, it's more effective to listen first and therefore calm down the other person's elephant. After that, you can gently guide the elephant to the right answer.

Principle #25:

Try to see the world from the other person's perspective, even if you know you're right. Your willingness to listen results in learning opportunities and increases the chance that you will successfully influence the other person.

This above helps you to positively influence other people, whether it's to get colleagues to take your ideas seriously or to persuade your boss that it's time for a salary raise. The next chapter will guide you through the steps to make this a reality.

CHAPTER 19:
THREE STEPS TO
INFLUENCE

When I had just started my career, I didn't know much about influence. I thought I could influence others by giving more arguments. I gave all the reasons why I was right, but the other side was still not convinced. I felt frustrated. I had ideas, but wasn't able to persuade others that those ideas were valuable. People listened but then moved on to the next topic.

This also happened when I worked on a consulting project for a consumer health multinational. While analyzing customer data, I discovered something interesting. The customers who were most likely to buy the company's products weren't interacting with the company's website content. I thought that by personalizing the content to this valuable group of customers, we could improve loyalty and revenue. I presented my findings with a suggestion on how to activate these customers.

Unfortunately, I made a few mistakes:

- As a rational person, I focused on facts, while people in front of me had a large emotional elephant. They weren't sensitive to dry numbers.

- I didn't tailor my arguments to the people in front of me. In fact, I had no idea what their goals were.

- When people didn't seem interested, I pushed even harder instead of finding out what would motivate them.

In other words, I didn't walk to the other side of the table. I made the same mistake over and over again — I kept arguing from my side, without considering how the other person looked at the situation.

Now we'll look at a three-step method to influence, which connects different parts from this book:

1) **BE SELF-AWARE:** Understand your own perspective.

2) **INTERACT:** Check the perspective of the other person.

3) **INFLUENCE:** Persuade the other person while considering the goals of the other person.

This process works particularly well in persuading someone when you have a certain goal or idea in mind. But be wary. From the interviews I conducted with analytical thinkers, I found that many people in this group make a crucial mistake and I'll tell you what it is. It's the same mistake that I made in the past.

But first, I'll show you the three steps and demonstrate the process through a practical example.

1. BE SELF-AWARE: Understand your own perspective

In the first step, you need to understand what's important to you.

Ask yourself:

- What is the context of this situation?
- Which of my algorithms play a role here?
- What are my personal goals?
- What emotions do I feel?
- What do I want to get out of the situation — when will I be satisfied?

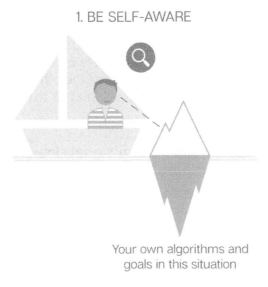

1. BE SELF-AWARE

Your own algorithms and
goals in this situation

2. INTERACT: Check the perspective of the other person

Now you have a solid understanding of what you want. Can you start persuading others? No, not so fast. Don't skip step 2, because it's a crucial one.

Knowing your own goals and what you want to get out of the situation is an important first step. However, you still need to figure out how the other person looks at the situation. Pushing for your own goals without taking the other person's goals into account isn't effective. Walk to the other side of the table and see the world from the other person's perspective. Ask, "What is important to you in this situation? What is your goal? When would you be satisfied?"

Spending lots of time interacting with the other person may seem like a waste of time. But in reality, this is a great investment for two reasons:

1) We get more insight into the goals of the other person.

When we know the personal goals of the other person in a situation, we can use those insights to influence the other person. As an analytical thinker, you may think: "I understand the situation already."

Still, it's wise to validate whether you indeed understand the perspective of the other person. Remember the two cognitive biases, the illusion of asymmetric insight and false consensus effect. They trick us into thinking we know others better than we think we do. While validating our understanding of the other person's goals, we may discover new insights that we can use to create a win-win situation.

2) Caring about the other person's goals lowers resistance.

If you only care about your own point of view, the other person is more likely to show resistance to your idea. These barriers of resistance are usually lower when you show that you care about the other person's goals.

How come? Again, because of our algorithms. People have algorithms that are triggered when others display selfish behavior. In prehistoric times, surviving wasn't certain. Therefore, selfish people were dangerous. Today, people are still sensitive to such behavior. When you show that you only care about your own goals, they will close their mind and not listen to your ideas.

In contrast, when you show consideration to the perspective of the other person, you build trust. This lowers resistance and opens the gate to influence. Consider the emotional impact of the situation on the other person. Such an empathetic approach will help you build the relationship and increases the chance that they will be in favor of your ideas. Therefore, make a connection between you and the other person and try to fully understand their perspective. Once you do, check whether your understanding is right. Say, "For you it's important that _____ (fill in the blank). Is that right?" Remember those two sentences. They are incredibly valuable, even if your goal is not to persuade the other person.

2. INTERACT

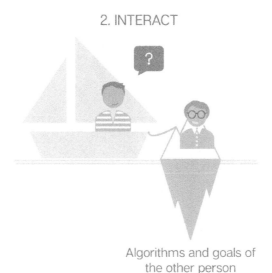

Algorithms and goals of
the other person

3. INFLUENCE: State your needs while considering the perspective of the other person

You explored your own perspective and decided what you want. After, you considered the perspective of the other person. Now, finally, you can start to influence the other person.

In this step, you will combine your knowledge from steps 1 and 2 to influence the other person. Be transparent about what you want, and why. Tell them how your idea will help them, or why it doesn't harm their personal goals. Do not overwhelm others with a mountain of statistics if they don't care about the data. Instead, appeal to personal goals and emotions.

Note: You cannot pull other people into your boat. You cannot force others to join your trip. However, you can make the boat attractive to them and make it easy to get on board. Lay out a comfortable bridge by highlighting how your idea will contribute to their personal goals.

There is a lot of literature on persuasion. If you are interested in learning more, I recommend you read the book *Influence* by Robert Cialdini.

3. INFLUENCE

Algorithms and goals of
the other person

In summary:

1) **BE SELF-AWARE:** First, we explore our own goals in the situation.

2) **INTERACT:** Second, we check whether we understand the goals of the other person.

3) **INFLUENCE:** Third, we persuade the other person by connecting our own goals to the goals of the other person.

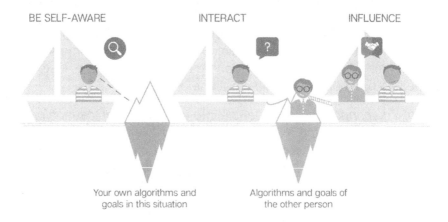

BE SELF-AWARE   INTERACT   INFLUENCE

Your own algorithms and   Algorithms and goals of
goals in this situation   the other person

Let me illustrate this process with a personal example. Do you recognize the three steps?

Be self-aware

When I moved to Barcelona in 2017, I tried to build new habits. Before coming to work, I wanted to go to the beach to work out. After my workout, I would have a quick swim and run back to my apartment. But there was one challenge: this routine would make me late to work. That's why I had to discuss it with the director. Let's call him David.

I could choose the easy way: let go of my ambition to work out in the morning. I could swallow my preferences and avoid a difficult conversation. However, I didn't want to be a nice guy. Instead, I wanted to be a MindSpeaker. I wanted to be transparent about my preferences while considering the needs of other people. Even though I felt an uncomfortable tension in my stomach, I decided to speak with David.

Interact

If I were to argue from my side of the table, I would probably say something along the lines of, "I want to work out in the morning because it makes me happy."

That looks rather self-centered, doesn't it?

When I walked over to the other side of the table, I got an idea of how David may look at the world:

- The office in Barcelona was brand new. David was building the business, and in this situation of uncertainty, he eagerly wanted to keep our clients happy. Damaging the relationship with one of our clients would harm the business significantly.

- David wanted me to perform well, especially since I was on an expensive foreign contract.

- If I did the workout in the morning, it would mean I arrived late to work, while other employees were expected to come in at the normal time. This could lead to other employees questioning David about giving me special treatment.

Interact + Influence

In my conversation with David, I validated these assumptions and tried to persuade him by framing my request from his side of the table. What did that look like?

Me: "I have a request. I'd like to work out in the morning before work, because I feel much more energetic and productive on those days. I want to discuss this with you, because if I do my workout in the morning, I would get to the office late. I have some ideas about your interests, but can you tell me what your needs are in this situation? Then we can explore how we can both get our needs met."

David: "I don't want this to have any negative impact on the customer."

Me: "I can imagine that it's important for you to keep our customers happy, especially in the first months at this new business location."

David: "Exactly. We shouldn't lose any of our ongoing consulting projects."

Me: "I see. What I can do is ask the customer if they're okay with me not being available at the start of the day. Then I'll make sure it doesn't impact the client's satisfaction. If it does, I will stop the workout. Would that help?"

David: "Yes."

Me: "Do you have any worries about me coming in later than the rest of the team?"

David: "No, that's fine. You're free to manage your own working hours."

Then, he added: "Actually, I want to go back to my morning workout too."

What followed was a personal conversation on how he used to have more time for his hobbies until his first child knocked on the door. It was a pleasant and interesting talk.

Wow. That was easy. How come? Figuratively, I walked over to his side of the table and addressed all of his goals and possible concerns. He felt understood and assured that there would be no impact.

Through this approach, I achieved two things:

1) I could start my morning workout. This made me both happier and more productive.

2) I showed that I cared about David's needs. That's why my request didn't harm the relationship. Rather, I built more trust with the most senior person in the office.

Many people are aware of what they want in step 1, then they jump to step 3 to influence the other person. Unfortunately, that means they skip the most important step: finding out what the other person wants.

Principle #26:

When you try to persuade someone: first understand your own goals, then understand the other person's goals, and finally propose your idea in a way that benefits both you and the other person. Spending enough time and energy on step 2, understanding the other person's perspective, increases your chances of successful persuasion.

Exercise #10:

■ *Want to persuade? Walk to the other side of the table.*

Next time you get into a situation where you want to persuade someone, walk to the other side of the table to interact with the other person. Ask questions to check whether you understand their goals. After the situation, reflect. What happened with the other person when you listened to their needs? What did the person say? What nonverbal behavior did you see?

When we want to persuade someone, often we don't spend enough time interacting. The same is true for other situations of influence. Don't focus so much on your own goals, your selfish arguments, your own point of view. Instead, walk to the other side of the table and focus on the other person's perspective. The next chapter demonstrates how you can do that in other situations of influence.

CHAPTER 20:
OTHER SITUATIONS OF INFLUENCE

This chapter demonstrates several situations in which you can benefit from walking to the other side of the table.

Want to sell?

Don't say how much time it took for you to build your product. Don't elaborate on the technical features either. Instead, say what benefits the product brings to the customer. Paint a vivid picture to illustrate how it will help them improve their life.

Do you want a salary raise? In that case, you're selling yourself. Don't complain that you worked so hard. Don't say that you want to get some extra money for your holiday to Brazil.

Instead, speak about what matters to the person in front of you. Tell them about the value you delivered in the past and how you expect to expand your contribution to the company in the future.

Want to negotiate?

Don't focus on the position. Instead, focus on the needs behind that position.

What does that mean?

Let's go back to the example where I ask David whether I can work out in the morning and arrive late in the office. To illustrate my point in this section, imagine that David isn't in favor of my request.

My position: I want to do sports in the morning.

David's position: I don't want Gilbert to do sports in the morning.

In such a negotiation, the pie is fixed:

1) I don't do sports in the morning. (I'm unhappy.)

2) I do sports in the morning. (David's unhappy.)

3) I do sports in the morning, but for only 30 minutes instead of an hour. I can't do a full workout and I'm still late to work. (We're both a bit unhappy.)

Result: at least one of us must compromise and therefore get a smaller piece of the pie.

What we need to realize is that in most situations, the size of the pie is not fixed.

When we understand the needs behind the other person's position, we can find ways to expand the pie. To understand the other person's needs, I need to walk to the other side of the table and understand their concern. Let's imagine in this case that David's needs are slightly different compared to the original example.

Gilbert's needs: I want to feel energized, happy, productive.

David's needs: I don't want to give Gilbert special treatment. I'm afraid that other people will start to complain about him coming in late.

Now we understand that David doesn't want me to come in late, we can look for an option C that meets both of our needs.

Through our creative problem-solving we find out that David has a gym membership close to the office. He can arrange a free membership for one month, outside of peak hours. Instead of sports in the morning, I could do my workout during lunchtime and benefit from the free membership. In that way, both of our needs are met. I can feel energized (my needs), and David doesn't need to deal with complaints about me coming in late (his needs). As a bonus, I can benefit from the free membership for a month.

Often, the size of the pie isn't fixed. The choice doesn't need to be solution A: meeting your needs or solution B: meeting the other person's needs. Seek solution C, which meets both interests. By understanding the needs behind the positions, you are able to expand the pie. If you keep on pressing for your own needs from your side of the table, you will be blind to these opportunities. If you want to read more about negotiation, I recommend reading the book *Getting to Yes* by Roger Fisher and William Ury.[37]

Want to solve a conflict?

When you are in a conflict, chances are that emotions have risen to the ceiling. You may feel anger, frustration, or irritation.

The more you feel your heartbeat in your chest and the blood pumping through your veins, the less likely you can see the situation objectively. The only thing you can see is your own point of view, how right you are, and how stupid the other person is for not seeing that.

While in conflict, it's hard to walk to the other side of the table. But if you do, it usually has a large effect. Once people feel heard and sense that you appreciate their ideas, they will become more open to your point of view.

Set aside your own arguments and start by listening empathetically. When the other person's elephant feels heard, he will calm down. Only then will you start making your own point, and only then will it be easier to guide the elephant in the right direction. In contrast, if you keep stressing your own needs without listening, the elephant will become even more stubborn. In summary, spend more time in step 2 of the process of influence: discovering the goals and emotions of the other person.

In situations of tension, the fight-or-flight response has a tendency to kick in. That's why it's hard to see the situation objectively. When you feel cornered, emotional, and unable to properly assess the situation, take a break. Pause. Breathe deeply a few times. That will help you calm down and see the situation more objectively. William Ury, founder of the negotiation program of Harvard Law School, calls this pause "going to the balcony."

In Part 2, we learned how to optimize our algorithms. This is exactly what we're doing here. Instead of letting our emotions control us, we decide how we respond to our emotions. We don't allow ourselves to judge the other person for being wrong, because such behavior will only escalate the situation. Instead, we take responsibility by considering: what can *I* do to improve the situation?

The answer to this question is, of course, walk to the other side of the table. Ask questions to find out what is most important to the other person. Then, say out loud: "For you, it's important that _____ [fill in the blank]. Is that right?" Once people see that you understand what is important to them, their emotional elephant will calm down. That's how you prevent a conflict from escalating and collectively create understanding instead.

Want to explain expert knowledge?

When you are explaining expert knowledge to someone else, you need to deal with the curse of knowledge.

A study at Stanford University illustrated the curse of knowledge through a game. People were either assigned the role of *tapper* or *listener*. The tappers received a well-known song like "Happy Birthday" and had to tap out the rhythm to a listener by knocking on the table. The listeners needed to guess which song it was.

Beforehand, the tappers needed to predict the percentage of songs that would be guessed correctly. On average, they predicted the odds to be 50%. In contrast, only 2.5% of the listeners guessed correctly.[38]

How come the tappers' predictions were so far from reality? When the tapper taps the song, they hear the song in their head. But at the same time, the listeners don't hear that melody. They only hear some knocks on the table.

The tappers are flabbergasted that people aren't able to guess the song. "Isn't it obvious?"

As a tapper, it's hard to imagine what it's like to hear only some meaningless taps instead of the recognizable melody. This is the curse of knowledge. Once we know something, it's difficult to imagine what it was like to not know it. The knowledge has "cursed" us.

Once we're knowledgeable on a topic, it's difficult to share that knowledge because it's tough to recreate the state of mind of our listeners.

How can we fight the curse of knowledge? By understanding the perspective of our audience: walk to the other side of the table. An IKEA table, to be specific.

Interest:

- What are they interested in? Don't dive into technical details. Instead, tell the audience how it will impact their work.

Knowledge:

- What do they already know? Tell them something new, but don't make it too difficult. This is a tricky balance.
- Stay away from jargon. Use words that they understand. Or even better, use words that they use.

Engage:

- What stories and examples would help to illustrate your key points?

Assumptions:

- Avoid assumptions about the audience's interest, knowledge level, and best way of engagement. Better to check beforehand than waste people's time.

When you explain expert knowledge, imagine that you are the tapper and the other person is the listener. Realize that the other person has a hard time understanding your explanation. Walk to the other side of the IKEA table to ensure you get your message across.

CONCLUSION PART 4

In the previous part of the book, we discussed how you can increase your influence. When you buy a new car, it comes with a user manual. But when you work with a new person, you need to figure everything out. That's why it's valuable to express how others can best work with you to give them the opportunity to change their behavior in your interests. You can express your preferences in two ways.

First, you can share your data proactively, before the behavior of the other person occurs. In other words, you tell them about your algorithms. In doing so, you educate them on what works well for you and what doesn't. You feed their brain with more data so they can learn and take your preferences into account. Another benefit of sharing more of your data is that you plant conversational seeds. These help others relate to you and develop a fun and productive conversation.

Second, you can share your data reactively, giving feedback to the other person. This helps the other person better understand your algorithms and maybe use that information to change their behavior in the future.

Be expressive about your algorithms, but always do so with empathy. It's important to realize that everyone has different preferences. Ask questions about their algorithms and listen well. Try to understand their view, no matter how much their preferences differ from yours. This interest in their algorithms helps you understand how you and the other person can best collaborate.

Next, this chapter explained a three-step process to influence other people:

1) Be self-aware

2) Interact

3) Influence

This process works particularly well in persuading someone when you have a certain goal or idea in mind. As I explained, many people don't spend enough time in step 2. This step feels unproductive and seems to delay the process, but usually the opposite is true. By walking to the other side of the table and understanding the perspective of the other person, you achieve two things:

1) You understand the interests behind the other person's position. This enables you to come up with ideas for a win-win solution.

2) Since you show that you care about the other person's goals, they're more likely to agree with your suggestions

When we use the three-step method to persuade others, we not only increase our chances of getting what we want, but we also build a strong relationship, instead of tearing it apart through dishonesty.

CONCLUSION

In this book, we spoke about discovering patterns in your own behavior and in the behavior of other people. Now, let's have a look at the patterns in this book.

While you read this conclusion, reflect on what you've learned. What key lessons did you take in? Have you discovered any of your own algorithms? Did you recognize any behavioral patterns in someone else?

Part 1 – BE SELF-AWARE: Understand Your Own Algorithms

The first part of this book was about understanding your own algorithms.

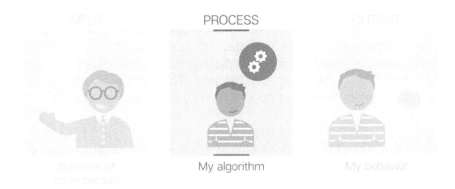

PROCESS

My algorithm

We started with emotional intelligence and the story about the emotional elephant and the rational rider; they need to work in harmony. Emotions play an important role in your life, even as a rational person. Emotions are useful pieces of information that can tell you a lot about yourself and about other people. Use that information to your advantage.

Thanks to evolution, our mind is irrationally sensitive to being liked and being part of a group. These fears are outdated but still vastly influence our decision-making.

You have built many algorithms, whether in your childhood or in recent years. Some of those algorithms are now running your life — for better or worse.

Part 2 – OPTIMIZE: Change Your Behavior

Part 2 discussed how you can change your behavior.

By continually choosing a new type of behavior, your algorithms automatically adjust. In other words, through consistent action, you reprogram your mind. We looked at changing your Joker algorithms, then examined how you can get the best out of your Batman algorithms. By positively influencing your surroundings, you create your own high-performing environment. This is how you minimize your Joker algorithms and maximize your Batman algorithms.

Part 3 – INTERACT: Understand Other People's Algorithms

Part 3 studied other people's algorithms.

PROCESS

Algorithm of
other person

You can observe behavior, but doing so will give you only information on the surface. By digging deeper and asking people about their algorithms, you get information about their beliefs and needs. Understanding these elements is crucial as they are the building blocks of each algorithm. In other words, they are the driving force of people's behavior. Algorithms can be described with the people skills formula:

- Person wants to get [NEED].
- Person thinks [BELIEF].
- That is why person does [BEHAVIOR].

People don't always behave in a way that we appreciate. We don't always understand that response either. But no matter how tempting, stay away from judging. Judging will only magnify the differences between you and the other person. By staying curious, you keep the connection. Also, this curiosity helps to identify what you can learn from people with a different personality.

With a deep understanding of the algorithms of others, you can accurately predict how others will respond to your behavior. However, the goal of developing such awareness is not to carefully choose the socially desirable behavior in order to please others. This strategy is based on the wrong understanding, because most people don't enjoy such nice guy behavior. Instead, become more expressive and don't be afraid to stand out. Take small steps and grow into a MindSpeaker.

Part 4 – INFLUENCE: Steer Other People's Behavior

Part 4 focused on influencing other people's behavior.

INPUT   PROCESS   OUTPUT

Your behavior   Algorithm of other person   Behavior of other person

When you understand the algorithms of other people, you understand the driving forces of their behavior. However, the goal is not to use this information to manipulate others. Instead, strive to create win-win situations that benefit all parties.

Sharing your algorithms helps people understand how they can best work with you. Always do so with empathy and try to understand the other person's perspective. That is key in the three-step process for influence too. Most people don't spend enough time discovering the other person's goals. They are too busy with their own goals. Walking to the other side of the table seems like a delay. However, often this additional step is the quickest road to successful persuasion.

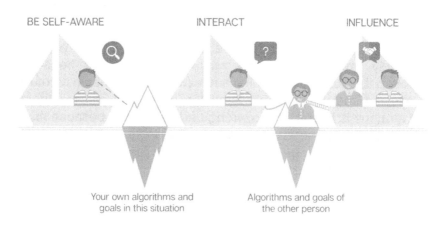

BE SELF-AWARE   INTERACT   INFLUENCE

Your own algorithms and goals in this situation   Algorithms and goals of the other person

THE NEXT STEP: DO YOU DARE TO LEAVE THE PARKING LOT?

Self-driving cars learn from new experiences.

Driving on an empty parking lot is easy, because there are few variables. Avoiding a collision with objects that don't move isn't rocket science. In such a simple situation, the car's algorithms don't improve.

Now, imagine a self-driving car in a crowded city center. The narrow streets, complex traffic rules, and numerous other moving vehicles increase the complexity of the decision-making. Thanks to these new experiences, the algorithms learn how to deal with new situations. As a result, the car's algorithms improve.

Your own algorithms learn in a similar way.

People find it easiest to deal with known situations. A beer with a friend — nothing new. Your uncle's birthday — you know what to expect. Lunch with a colleague at your favorite place — the usual, please. Your algorithms know exactly what your behavior should be. These situations are comfortable, but opportunities to improve your social skills are scarce.

In contrast, when you get into settings you are unfamiliar with, the potential for learning is limitless.

- Are you starting a project with a colleague who you had trouble collaborating with in the past?
- Do you have a new manager whose personality is the opposite of yours?
- Have you been invited to a housewarming party where you won't know anyone?

Uncomfortable situations.

Beautiful opportunities.

These different interactions feed your personal algorithms with new data. And this is what helps your algorithms improve. Each new situation trains your algorithms on what works and what does not.

New situations can be daunting. But only if you dare to expose yourself will your people skills improve.

Get into the social jungle. Experiment. Fail. Because doing so gives you more data for future decisions.

What car do you want to be?

A lousy one that's only able to drive in an empty parking lot?

Or a car that learns to deal with more complex situations and slowly but steadily grows into a self-driving Ferrari?

You decide.

FINAL WORDS

You did it.

You belong to a small group on this large globe. Many people say they want to improve their people skills, but few are willing to put the effort into making this wish a reality.

I sincerely hope this book has been helpful to you. Reading this book may be a small or big step in boosting your people skills. In any case, don't let it be your last. Remember, becoming more self-aware and advancing your people skills is a never-ending process. I would like to help you take the next step.

Soft Skills for Data & Analytics professionals

That feeling, as a Data Scientist or Analyst, when people don't use your data products. Or when they don't act on your data insights. Join my next interactive workshop and see the results of your hard data work.

➤ mindspeaking.com/training

Discover the 4 mindsets & 3 key communication skills

Do you work in data & analytics? Based on insights from 62 leaders, I created the Mindspeaking Maturity Model. My goal is to help you grow. What's your maturity level? Find out your now:

➤ mindpeaking.com/maturity-model

Let's stay connected via LinkedIn. Or say hi via email: Gilbert@MindSpeaking.com

Thank you. I'm honored that you have read my work.

Looking forward to MindSpeaking with you,

Gilbert

ACKNOWLEDGMENTS

My name is the only name on the cover. But is that fair? I could never have written this book without the tremendous support of the people around me.

My appreciation goes out to:

Katharina, thank you for inspiring me to write more. Our conversation in New Zealand was the trigger. I will never forget that. This book would not exist without you.

Many thanks to all my friends, family, and people in my professional network who helped me create this book. Special thanks go out to the people who provided feedback on draft versions of this book: Matthias, Nelis, Rik, Joost, Niek 3, Bard, Erik, Neal, Rob, Stendert, Quido, Gijs, Alexander, Mariano, Bogdan, Saby, Angela, Gert, Menno, Arne, Mikael, Remco, Alexandre, Arjen, Sina, Mohamed, Sujith, Martin, Tuur, Shairoz, Rick, David, Martin, Pieter, and Thomas. Also, I want to share my appreciation for Hans and Jo. While they didn't directly contribute to the book, they helped me to grow into the person who I am today.

Lisa Kroes, thank you for designing the awesome illustrations. I'm sure your company will be a great success. Ameesha Green, your first name means "pure" and "truthful." That is what your feedback was like, difficult to take in, but invaluable in improving the book. Thanks for being such a professional editor. Stacey, thank you for your detailed editing work and improving that last 2%.

Then, I want to thank my parents. Dad, thank you for always taking care of me. What feels ordinary for you has been an outstanding help for me. Mom, thank you for stimulating my creative side. You didn't give up, even after I told you for the hundredth time: "I am not creative." I think I've changed my mind.

Lastly, Lena, thank you for your never-ending support. You gave me the freedom to work on this book. I am grateful that you understand how much this book matters to me. Even when that meant I sat behind my laptop instead of spending time with you. You kept asking me, "How can I help you be productive?" Especially in the most difficult writing phases, your optimism pushed me forward. Muito obrigado. Muchas gracias. I love you.

ABOUT THE AUTHOR

As a former professional poker player, you can find Gilbert Eijkelenboom wherever psychology and data meet. While my academic background is in Behavioral Science, I've built a career in Data & Analytics.

Combining both worlds, I founded the company MindSpeaking: soft skills training for Data & Analytics.

Data & Analytics professionals are smart people with great ideas.

I believe their ideas should be heard.

Unfortunately, many insights and data products are never used by the business.

My mission is to help Data & Analytics professionals become confident communicators, so that they get the best out of the data and the best out of themselves.

REFERENCES

1. "Soft skills." *Cambridge Dictionary.* Accessed 28 July, 2020. *https://dictionary.cambridge.org/us/dictionary/english/soft-skills.*

2. Volini, Erica, Jeff Schwartz, Indranil Roy, Maren Hauptmann, Yves Van Durme, Brad Denny, and Josh Bersin. *2019 Deloitte Global Human Capital Trends: Reinvent with Human Focus.* New York: Deloitte Development, 2019. https://www2.deloitte.com/content/dam/Deloitte/cz/Documents/human-capital/cz-hc-trends-reinvent-with-human-focus.pdf.

3. "2018 Workplace Learning Report." *LinkedIn Learning.* Accessed July 25, 2020. https://learning.linkedin.com/resources/workplace-learning-report-2018.

4. Bughin, Jacques, Eric Hazan, Susan Lund, Peter Dahlström, Anna Wiesinger, and Amresh Subramaniam. "Skill shift: Automation and the future of the workforce." *McKinsey Global Institute.* May 23, 2018. https://www.mckinsey.com/featured-insights/future-of-work/skill-shift-automation-and-the-future-of-the-workforce.

5. Börner, Katy, Olga Scrivner, Mike Gallant, Shutian Ma, Xiaozhong Liu, Keith Chewning, Lingfei Wu, and James A. Evans. "Skill Discrepancies Between Research Education, and Jobs Reveal the Critical Need to Supply Soft Skills for the Data Economy." *Proceedings of the National Academy of Sciences* 115, no. 50 (December 2018): 12630-12637. https://doi.org/10.1073/pnas.1804247115.

6. Kahneman, Daniel. *Thinking, Fast and Slow.* New York: Farrar, Straus and Giroux, 2013.

7. Haidt, Jonathan. *The Happiness Hypothesis: Finding Modern Truth in Ancient Wisdom.* New York: Basic Books, 2005.

8. Langlois, Richard N. "Bounded Rationality and Behavioralism: A Clarification and Critique." *Journal of Institutional and Theoretical Economics* 146, no. 4, (1990): 691-695. https://richard-langlois.uconn.edu/wp-content/uploads/sites/1617/2019/09/JITE_1990.pdf.

9. Goleman, Daniel. *Emotional Intelligence.* New York: Bantam Books, 1997.

10. Damasio, Antonio R. *Descartes' Error: Emotion, Reason, and the Human Brain.* New York: Avon Books, 1994.

11. Bradberry, Travis. *Emotional Intelligence 2.0.* San Diego: TalentSmart, 2009.

12. Leary, Mark R. "Toward a Conceptualization of Interpersonal Rejection." In *Interpersonal Rejection,* edited by Mark Leary, 3-20. New York: Oxford University Press, 2001.

13. Bowlby, John. *Attachment.* New York: Basic Books, 1969.

14. Eurich, Tasha. *Insight: Why We're Not As Self-aware As We Think, and How Seeing Ourselves Clearly Helps Us Succeed At Work and in Life.* New South Wales: Currency, 2017.

15. Kruger, Justin, and David Dunning. "Unskilled and Unaware of It: How Difficulties in Recognizing One's Own Incompetence Lead to Inflated Self-Assessments. *Journal of Personality and Social Psychology* 77, no. 6, (January, 2000): 1121-1134. https://doi.org/10.1037//0022-3514.77.6.1121.

16. Smith, Timothy W., Bert N. Uchino, Cynthia A. Berg, Paul Florsheim, Gale Pearce, Melissa Hawkins, Paul N. Hopkins, and Hyo-chun Yoon. "Hostile Personality Traits and Coronary Artery Calcification in Middle-Aged and Older Married Couples: Different Effects for Self-Reports Versus Spouse-Ratings." Psychosomatic Medicine 69, no. 5, (June, 2007): 441–448. https://doi/10.1097/PSY.0b013e3180600a65.

17. Wilson, Timothy D. *Strangers to Ourselves: Discovering the Adaptive Unconscious.* Cambridge: Harvard University Press, 2004.

18. Lally, Phillippa, Cornelia H. M. van Jaarsveld, Henry W. W. Potts, and Jane Wardle. "How are habits formed: Modelling habit formation in the real world." *European Journal of Social Psychology* 40, no. 6, (July 2009): 998-1009. https://doi.org/10.1002/ejsp.674.

19. Reina, Dennis, and Michelle Reina. *Trust and betrayal in the workplace: Building Effective Relationships in your Organization.* Oakland: Berrett-Koehler, 2015.

20. Maslow, A.H. "A theory of human motivation." *Psychological Review* 50 (1943): 370-396. http://psychclassics.yorku.ca/ Maslow/motivation.htm.

21. Tamir, Diana L., and Jason P. Mitchell. "Disclosing information about the self is intrinsically rewarding." *Proceedings of the National Academy of Sciences* 109, no. 21, (February, 2012): 8038–8043. https://doi.org/10.1073/pnas.1202129109.

22. Covey, Stephen M. R. *The Speed of Trust: The One Thing That Changes Everything.* Read by Stephen M. R. Covey. New York: Simon & Schuster Audio, 2006. Audiobook, 12 hr., 13 min.

23. Hampton, Adam J., Amanda N. Fisher Boyd, and Susan Sprecher. "You're Like Me and I Like You: Mediators of the Similarity-Liking Link Assessed Before and After a Getting-Acquainted Social Interaction." *Journal of Social and Personal Relationships* 36, no. 7 (July, 2018): 2221-2244. https://doi. org/10.1177/0265407518790411.

24. Willis, Janine, and Alexander Todorov. "First Impressions: Making Up Your Mind After a 100-MS Exposure to a Face." *Psychological Science* 17, no. 7, (July, 2006): 592–598. https:// doi.org/10.1111/j.1467-9280.2006.01750.x.

25. Pazzaglia, Mariella. "Body and Odors: Not Just Molecules, After All." *Current Directions in Psychological Science* 24, (August, 2015): 329-333. https://doi.org/10.1177/0963721415575329.

26. Wason, P. C. "On the Failure to Eliminate Hypotheses in a Conceptual Task." *Quarterly Journal of Experimental Psychology* 12, (April, 2008): 129–140.https://doi. org/10.1080/17470216008416717.

27. Darley, John M., and Paget H. Gross. "A Hypothesis-Confirming Bias In Labeling Effects." *Journal of Personality and Social Psychology* 44, no. 1 (1983): 20-33.https://doi. org/10.1037/0022-3514.44.1.20.

28. Greene, Robert. *The Laws of Human Nature.* New York: Viking, 2018.

29. Kegan, Robert, and Lisa Laskow Lahey. *Immunity to Change: How to Overcome It and Unlock the Potential in Yourself and Your Organization.* Cambridge: Harvard Business Review Press, 2009.

30. Hollman, Wayne A., and Brian H. Kleiner. "Establishing Rapport: The Secret Business Tool to Success." *Managing Service Quality* 7, no. 4 (August, 1997): 194-197. https://doi.org/10.1108/09604529710173015.

31. Glover, Robert A. *No More Mr. Nice Guy: A Proven Plan for Getting What You Want in Love, Sex, and Life.* Philadelphia: Running Press, 2003.

32. Brooks, David. *The Social Animal: The Hidden Sources of Love, Character, and Achievement.* New York: Random House, 2011.

33. Asch, S. E. "Effects of Group Pressure upon the Modification and Distortion of Judgments." In *Groups, Leadership and Men; Research in Human Relations,* by Harold Guetzkow, 177-190. Pittsburgh: Carnegie Press, 1951.

34. Sprecher, Susan, Stansilav Treger, Joshua D. Wondra, Nicole Hilaire, and Kevin Wallpe. "Taking Turns: Reciprocal Self-Disclosure Promotes Liking in Initial Interactions." *Journal of Experimental Social Psychology* 49, no. 5, (2013): 860–866. https://doi.org/10.1016/j.jesp.2013.03.017.

35. Pronin, Emily, Justin Kruger, Kenneth Savitsky, and Lee Ross. "You Do Not Know Me, But I Know You: The Illusion Of Asymmetric Insight." *Journal of Personality & Social Psychology* 81, no. 4 (October, 2001): 639-656. https://doi.org/10.1037/0022-3514.81.4.639/.

36. Ross, Lee, David Greene, and Pamela House. "The False Consensus Effect: An Egocentric Bias in Social Perception and Attribution Processes." *Journal of Experimental Social Psychology* 13, no. 3, (1997): 279-301. https://doi.org/10.1016/0022-1031(77)90049-X.

37. Fisher, Roger, and Bruce Patton. *Getting to Yes: Negotiating Agreement without Giving In,* 3rd ed. London: Penguin Books, 2011.

38. Newton, Elizabeth Louise "The Rocky Road from Actions to Intentions." Unpublished PhD diss., Stanford University, 1990.

Made in the USA
Monee, IL
24 April 2022

95317800R00096